The Genus *Cornus*

DOGWOODS

Paul Cappiello
& Don Shadow

TIMBER PRESS
Portland · Cambridge

Half title page: *Cornus florida* 'Cherokee Chief'; frontispiece and title page: *C. kousa* 'Milky Way'; dedication (opposite): *C. kousa* var. *chinensis*

Published in 2005 by

Timber Press, Inc.
The Haseltine Building
133 S.W. Second Avenue, Suite 450
Portland, Oregon 97204-3527, U.S.A.

Timber Press
2 Station Road
Swavesey
Cambridge CB4 5QJ, U.K.

www.timberpress.com

Printed in China
Designed by Susan Applegate

Library of Congress Cataloging-in-Publication Data

Cappiello, Paul.
    Dogwoods: the genus Cornus / Paul Cappiello.
        p. cm.
    Includes bibliographical references and index.
    ISBN 0-88192-679-5 (hardcover)
    1. Cornus (Plants) I. Title.
    QK495.C785C37 2005
    635.9'77384–dc22   2004019080

A catalog record for this book is also available from the British Library.

To my parents,
Carol and Vincent Cappiello,

who taught by example how to live a good life;
one deed at a time,
one friend at a time,
and one day at a time.

PAUL CAPPIELLO

CONTENTS

9 Preface & Acknowledgments

15 Introduction

23 **Chapter 1. The Family** *Cornaceae*

23 Dogwood Characteristics

28 Dogwood Breeding and Selection

32 Insect and Disease Problems

39 **Chapter 2. The** *Cornus canadensis* **Group**

39 *Cornus canadensis*

45 *Cornus suecica*

45 *Cornus ×unalaschkensis*

47 **Chapter 3. The** *Cornus alba* **Group**

49 *Cornus alba*

57 *Cornus amomum*

58 *Cornus asperifolia*

59 *Cornus australis*

59 *Cornus bretschneideri*

59 *Cornus glabrata*

60 *Cornus obliqua*

60 *Cornus oblonga*

61 *Cornus paucinervis*

61 *Cornus pumila*

62 *Cornus racemosa*

66 *Cornus rugosa*

66 *Cornus sanguinea*

70 *Cornus sessilis*

70 *Cornus stolonifera*

80 *Cornus walteri*

83　**Chapter 4. The *Cornus alternifolia* Group**
84　*Cornus alternifolia*
87　*Cornus controversa*
93　*Cornus macrophylla*

97　**Chapter 5. The *Cornus florida* Group**
97　*Cornus florida*
138　*Cornus angustata*
140　*Cornus capitata*
142　*Cornus kousa*
185　*Cornus nuttallii*
189　*Cornus florida* Group Hybrids

201　**Chapter 6. The *Cornus mas* Group**
201　*Cornus mas*
209　*Cornus chinensis*
209　*Cornus officinalis*

213　Glossary
214　Bibliography
215　USDA Hardiness Zone Map
217　Index

Cornus kousa 'Bush's Pink'

PREFACE & ACKNOWLEDGMENTS

THERE IS A COLOR BLUE n the northern winter sky, a color that only comes late in the evening, when the sun is almost gone, on those nights so cold that the new snow on the ground crunches beneath your feet like little puffs of Styrofoam™. I've not seen this color anywhere else. I don't even know what name would be assigned to it by a painter. It is just one of those unique, all-too-infrequent glimpses into a world we, thankfully, will never fully comprehend; however, the lifelong quest for a little better understanding and a little greater appreciation is a worthy life's goal indeed. It is certainly one of the things that keeps me going, through all the unimportant clutter that tries to interrupt each and every day.

So in this book, I am not trying to unravel the meaning of life. Rather, my modest goal is to simply add something to our little corner of understanding of the big picture. Some writers write on philosophy. Others add to the world of physics, mathematics, history, physiology, or music. Each adds a chapter to the story. If one could only take it all in. Maybe one day, on my next vacation perhaps, I'll have enough time to read all those books piled next to my bed.

Another quest missing from the pages of this book is an overt attempt to save the planet in one fell swoop . . . if every person on the globe would just plant one dogwood per year for their entire life, we would reverse global warming, save the whales, and figure out how to turn spent nuclear waste into high quality chocolate! Not exactly my style.

My formal training is in both environmental planning and design, and horticulture, but primarily, I am a gardener. I grew up in a gardening family of six kids.

We always had gardens. Vegetable gardens. Flower gardens. Even woodland gardens we called freeforms (large, boulder-lined areas planted with whatever we found in the woods). On Mother's Day, we always went to church and on the way home stopped by the nursery to let my mother pick out a few plants. We then went home and worked in her gardens all day, mulching, pruning, even creating new gardens. Believe it or not, in the how's-this-for-a-universal-twist realm, the first tree I ever planted was a flowering dogwood dug out of the woods behind our house during one of these family gardening events. Of course, that was before we knew wild harvest to be a significant horticultural no-no. It is amazing how things change. (I remember reading once in a 1960s extension circular that digging plants out of the local woods was a good thing to do because it guaranteed that your plant was well adapted to the local area!)

No, there is no question about it. I am first and foremost a gardener. So what are the goals of this work? My answer is several-fold and more or less follows what has motivated my teaching and research career as well as my work in public horticulture.

First is to share my love of the wondrous diversity of the natural world. I am continuously amazed by the subtle and elegant beauty in the simplest things. My wife sometimes uses the word *simpleton*, but that is another story. Mother Nature just seems to know how to pull it all together. An artfully sculpted tree situated proudly on a rocky point, perfectly framing the view of an island beyond. The bold trace of lichens over a granite boulder. Morning light on a grassy meadow. I am certainly not the only one who feels the tug between intelligent design and evolutionary happenstance.

The second goal in writing this book is to share my love of exploration. Not the exploration of space or the nanoworld but exploration of the plant world. I don't understand physics. I don't understand astronomy. I don't have that gene. I do have a plant gene though, and ever since I was a kid, I've had this desire to understand why things are as they are and if there was some effective way to change the way things appeared. As a kid, I spent one entire summer trying to graft stems of a hanging basket of *Helichrysum* to the *Tradescantia* hanging next to it. I stripped leaves, wounded stems, used miles of my father's electrical tape, and as it turns out, practiced what I would later learn to be approach grafts, veneer grafts, nurse grafts, and whip-and-tongue grafts. I never made any progress but had great fun doing it.

My 10-year-old son has the bug, too, but he's got the physics-engineering gene. I don't know where it came from; there isn't an engineer in the Cappiello lineage for about 600 years, but he has it just the same. Fortunately for my childhood, experimentation with plants normally did not burn down the house, knock out power to the entire neighborhood, or attempt to attract lightening to the garage roof to create diamonds from coal. But let's not go there. My son really is a good kid and anyway, our house is still standing . . . for now.

My third goal in these pages is to make some worthy addition to the world of horticultural knowledge. I have long had an interest in what I call horticultural sociology. Not just the history of where plants originated, but the story behind the people and the circumstances. I have tried in this volume to include as many of these stories, or at least references, as was practical. Every day, we must lose hundreds of these plant history stories to the passing of the patriarchs and matriarchs of the plant world. And unfortunately, once the individuals are gone, the information they carry often goes with them. It is a sad state of the business that we have let so much go.

Finally, my approach in this book has been from the standpoint of and for the benefit of the gardener. I make no attempt to rewrite the taxonomic treatment of the genus *Cornus*. I have no desire to rewrite the natural history of the genus. Any such indication in the following pages is simply due to my inability as a writer. I hope simply to provide some information, possibly a little inspiration and a bit of enjoyment.

A work like this is seldom, if ever, a solitary endeavor. The notes, observations, and unrelated musings contained in these pages represent work that was made possible by many generous and knowledgeable people. I have never met a good plant person who was not at least a moderately opinionated individual. Most of the best carry opinion service to the level of high art. I have been fortunate to learn at the side of some of the best . . . and most opinionated. To those many, many gardeners who have shared their considered opinions and varied experiences, I thank you all for the majority of plant knowledge I have assembled over my gardening life. Knowledge is certainly the best pass-along plant of all.

It has been an honor and a privilege to write this book with Don Shadow. Longtime grower of dogwoods, he grew up in one of the family nurseries that was at the forefront of dogwood improvement. Through his lifetime, Don has become known worldwide as the keeper of as much plant knowledge as just about anyone on the planet. Much of the historical information contained in these pages was gleaned from conversations while walking nursery rows, over the phone, and rarely in Don's office. Without his input, this volume would have been sorely lacking.

I would like to thank Bruce Hamilton, Rutgers University, for planting the seed of horticulture as a profession and for serving as my first mentor in the world of horticulture; Michael Dirr, longtime friend and fellow bad driver, who shares with me the love of jumping highway medians to find the next great plant, to whom I will be eternally grateful for inspiration, guidance, and friendship; and Bill Mitchell, University of Maine, friend and colleague who endured countless hours in pouring rain and biting black flies while I took about 100,000 versions of my "very best slide ever."

Certainly the biggest "thank you" and "I love you" go to my wife, Carolyn, and son, Christopher, for their support and understanding and for putting up with "just one more weekend and it will be done."

Finally, to the Timber Press team and especially Neal Maillet, who as executive editor artfully guided this project through what might some day be known as the straits of eternity.

Happy Gardening!

PAUL CAPPIELLO

Cornus florida

INTRODUCTION

WHERE DOES ONE BEGIN with the dogwoods? From the battlefields of ancient Troy to the most humble and celebrated gardens, to modern molecular biology, the dogwoods have touched our history through the ages and are among the most recognizable of the plant kingdom's treasures.

Of course, in penultimate position sits one of the top dogs of the garden-plant world, the flowering dogwood, *Cornus florida*. A singular specimen in bloom seems quite enough to break the wretched hold of Hades and allow Persephone to ascend once again, bringing spring to a bleak and barren winter landscape. Along with gardeners the world over, we delight with Demeter at the sight of her beloved daughter's return from the underworld. And who's to say that the exquisite flowering dogwood is not the cause of such happenings?

Beyond the world of the ethereal, dogwoods have figured central to the march of civilization in many ways. *Cornus mas* was said to have provided the wood used by Odysseus and his men to build the Trojan horse and finally wrestle victory from the hands of defeat. The branches that were too small to provide lumber were used as arrow shafts. Of course, anyone who has ever grown the species might wonder if the wooden equine wasn't more legend than legit considering the shrubby nature of the plant.

In the world of pharmacognosy, it seems the dogwoods have saved us from many nasty ailments. According to the 1827 *Materia Medica*,

> the bark is tonic, astringent, and stimulating; it is given in powder, infusions, and decoctions. The stomach and bowels are sometimes disordered by it, and on this account it is generally combined with laudanum. It is

15

used in all diseases of debility, in agues, colic, and is combined with other tonics and aromatics: the dose is (2 scruples) of the powder.

Now would that be considered a drug or a food supplement? If we could just figure out what a scruple was!

Being extremely dense in composition, the wood of *Cornus florida* was used for everything from weaving shuttles to splitting wedges and finally, its most lucrative use of all, golf clubs. Thankfully, titanium and gullible golfers came along and, alas, the dogwoods have been spared.

Historically, some European species have been cultivated for centuries. The fruit of *Cornus mas* was fermented by the Greeks and Romans into what one can only imagine to have been a rather modest concoction. Several North American native peoples used the fruit of *C. canadensis* as a significant carbohydrate source during lean times of the year. From the taste of the pulp and its impact on the digestive tract, times must have been quite lean indeed.

Cornus mas. From *The Herball* by John Gerard (1597).

As ornamentals, the tree species have consistently been the big winners of gardeners' affections. Almost immediately after the first ships returned to England from the New World, seedlings of *Cornus florida* began showing up in British nursery catalogs. And lest we think too highly of ourselves these days, in all our modern new-plant enthusiasm, the pink-bracted *C. florida* was first described by the venerable plant collector Mark Catesby, way back in 1731! Unfortunately, while much sought after by gardeners of that time, the species just seems to need a bit more thermal encouragement than it often receives in England. In fact, celebrated English plantsman Christopher Lloyd was once taken to write of the species in England, "I prefer to visit it!" Enough said.

When British, Dutch, and German plant collectors first hit Asian soil, things really started to heat up for the dogwoods. And all the Heisman Trophy winners of the plant collecting world were in on the act: John G. Veitch, Philipp von Siebold, Ernest "Chinese"

Wilson, Reginald Farrer, and others. The floodgates opened up with *Cornus kousa*, *C. macrophylla*, *C. controversa*, *C. capitata*, and more. And the rest has been garden history.

Dogwoods have been with us since the time of the dinosaurs and have moved over most of the Northern Hemisphere and occasionally south of the equator as well. In the present-day plant world, *Cornus* species are known from Venezuela (*C. peruviana*) to subarctic North America (*C. canadensis*, *C. suecica*), across to Europe (*C. sanguinea*), and through much of Asia (*C. kousa*, *C. marcophylla*).

Taxonomy and nomenclature of the genus *Cornus* have been much debated over the centuries. Carl Linnaeus proposed the genus name in his 1753 *Species Plantarum*. The Latin word *cornus*, meaning "of the horn," is the ancient name for the tree. Since Linnaeus's time, there seems to have been a generalized jailbreak of nomenclatural silliness. Dividing the genus into multiple subgenera has kept plant taxonomists busy and tenured for some time. Is it a subspecies, species, or botanical variety? One could go on forever. Remember, put three taxonomists and a plant in a room and what do you get? Four new genera. To be fair, however, accurate plant taxonomy does have its place. It is essential to understanding evolution, plant geography, and myriad other natural history subjects.

To the gardener, plant taxonomy can also be a tremendous aid to identification, culture, and care. Consider the ericaceous plants (members of the family *Eri-*

Cornus florida. From *Histoire des plantes* by Henri Baillon (1867–1895).

caceae). Just knowing a plant is in this family will immediately inform that it will likely require acidic soil. Likewise, it is not worth your money to fertilize the plant with nitrate nitrogen as most members of the family are incapable of metabolizing the nitrate to ammonium, the nitrogen form useable by most plants.

Although Paul has studied a great deal of plant taxonomy, first and foremost, he is a plantsman, gardener, horticulturist, not plant taxonomist. And as important as plant classification can be to gardeners, it can also lead them astray. After all, the taxonomist and gardener walk to different drummers and require different shot for their shells. The plant taxonomist follows evolutionary relationships, similarities in reproductive biology, even those relationships based on molecular genetics. To the gardener, the perfect classification system would break plants into related groups based on cultural similarity and more gardenesque characteristics. Still some of the botanical classifications can seem absurd.

Consider the proposal of some taxonomists to lump *Cornus mas* and *C. canadensis* into their own subgenus. The former is a large woody shrub to tree, native to a wide range of natural conditions, tremendously adaptable, and lacking the showy large white floral bracts of many of the most ornamental *Cornus* species. The latter is a rhizomatous, herbaceous perennial with large showy white bracts that lives in highly acidic, moist soils and frustrates even the most talented of gardeners. It is a little like those $6.99 cheap-o dinner buffets families go to when the kids grow to the point where daily they eat 50 percent of their body weight in junk food. Such establishments always have some mystery product, swimming in a dark, presumably gravy-like substance. And if you are not paying attention, say while trying to keep your five-year-old from mixing chocolate pudding, mashed potatoes, and orange juice, you may absentmindedly put some of that mystery meat on your plate. And later, at the table, while distracted by your child who is now trying to see if he can create an explosion by mixing orange soda and black pepper and sprinkling it on the candle, you may, without thinking of it, actually eat some of this mystery offering. You might even be thinking that it doesn't taste half bad, until you look

Cornus canadensis. From *How Plants Grow* by Asa Gray (1860).

across the table to see the astonished look on your wife's face. It is only then, when she asks you what you are *doing*, that you realize, you have no idea what you have in your mouth. Oh what a place to be.

Now Paul has read the taxonomic literature. He's read it over and over again. But when his students ask him why *Cornus mas* and *C. canadensis* are sometimes placed in the same subgenus, he can almost taste the mystery meat all over again.

One option for handling the classification issue in this book was to ignore it altogether and simply list the species alphabetically. A coward's way out in my (Paul's) opinion. One that would miss the opportunity to inform. The second option was to follow the most current taxonomic treatment, if one could determine which treatment that would be. Possibly a sound academic exercise but likely of little value to gardeners. The third option was to come up with a system that would communicate something of value to gardeners. For better or worse, this is the path I have chosen for this work. The taxonomists have scores of textbooks and journals that treat the genus in *their* realm. To date, this is the only work on *Cornus* devoted entirely to the gardening use of the genus. It seems information of use to the gardener should be paramount. And so it shall. This is not meant to serve as a taxonomic revision of the genus *Cornus*. Rather the plants are arranged in such a way that gardeners will hopefully gain some better understanding by the arrangement of the information presented.

Finally, we turn to the treatment of plant names—not their conceptual categorization in the world of taxonomy, but the names and how they are presented in this book. Genus and species are relatively straightforward, as in *Cornus officinalis*. It is when we move to the cultivars, trademark names, varieties, and forms that the fog begins to close in.

Within any particular species, traits range to varying degrees around what we like to call typical. In a *variety* or *subspecies*, we see a group of plants that show a specific trait that sets the group apart from the rest of the species. In such a group, this trait is maintained through subsequent seed generations. Often times, varieties arise out of geographic isolation of a particular population of a species. An example of a variety is *Cornus florida* var. *rubra*, the pink-bracted flowering dogwood. If one grows seedlings from a pink-bracted parent, a healthy percentage will show pink bracts.

In a *form*, or more correctly *forma*, we see a group of plants with a trait that shows up occasionally throughout a population, generally at unpredictable rates of occurrence. An example in dogwoods is *Cornus florida* f. *xanthocarpa*, the yellow-fruited flowering dogwood. No matter your source of seed, if you grow enough seedlings, you will eventually come across a few yellow-fruited plants.

A *cultivar* is a group of plants that maintains its unique characteristic and is distinguishable from the species by some identifiable trait. Cultivars can be propagated sexually (seed) or asexually (vegetative). In the latter case, each plant is a clone of the original. These days, most woody plant cultivars are in fact clones, exact genetic copies of one another. Many of our annual plant cultivars (bedding plants, for example) are seed-produced cultivars. They simply arise from seed stock that has been bred to be homozygous for a particular trait or set of traits.

Assuming that the previous is somewhat clearer than day-old coffee, now we get into the confusing part. The world of patented plants and trademark names has increasingly caused gardeners all matter of frustration in recent years. The abridged version of how this all works is as follows. Any person or company that actively develops a new cultivar may patent that plant through the U.S. Patent and Trademark Office. The patent owner may then license any grower to propagate and sell specimens of that patented plant. Of course, this license typically carries with it a royalty payment to the patent's owner. Therefore, there is a certain profit incentive to develop and patent plants. Finally, when a plant is patented, it is usually patented under its cultivar name. The patent protection lasts for 25 years, after which anyone can propagate the plant without payment of royalties.

Now here comes the fun part. An individual or company may also register or claim a *trademark name*. Such names are denoted by ® for a registered mark or ™ for a nonregistered mark. These names are not directly tied to the plant. They are simply marketing names controlled by the trademark owner. As with a patent holder, a trademark owner may license use of that mark to others, usually for a fee. Trademark protection of a name can be extended indefinitely, giving it a huge long-term profit advantage over a patent. The trick is that one cannot patent a plant using a trademarked name. So what we end up with is plants patented under a nonsense or less-inspiring name but marketed and sold under a nice fancy trademark name. Thus, two names for the same plant as in *Cornus alternifolia* 'Wstackman' Golden Shadows™. It is not much of a system, but it is the one we have and must use. For a parallel, think of ibuprofen, marketed as Advil® and all its pharmaceutical brethren.

In this volume, cultivars, forms, and varieties are arranged alphabetically under each species. Any trademark names are listed with the appropriate cultivar.

Cornus kousa 'Greensleeves'

CHAPTER 1

THE FAMILY
Cornaceae

DOGWOODS, AS A GROUP, belong to the taxonomic family *Cornaceae*. Historically, this family has included *Cornus* and other genera of familiar ornamentals such as *Alangium*, *Aucuba*, *Davidia*, *Helwingia*, and *Nyssa*, among numerous genera less familiar to gardeners. Current taxonomic treatments of the family include as few as one genus (*Cornus*) to as many as 17 genera. The number of *Cornus* species generally ranges from 45 to 65 depending on who holds the stage. Readers interested in sorting through this academic challenge are invited to start with the references at the back of the book.

Dogwood Characteristics

Most garden reference books love to list dogwoods (at least *Cornus florida* and *C. kousa*) as the penultimate four-season plants in the landscape: spring flowers, summer fruit and foliage, autumn fruit and leaf color, and winter bark and form. In fact the supermarket checkout-stand gardening magazines have made such comments downright cliché. Yet if one is trying to capture the essence of the dogwoods, it is hard to avoid joining such unimaginative company. Ounce for ounce, dogwoods add more to the full season of the garden than just about any other group of garden plants.

Growth Habit

Dogwoods range from medium-sized trees to multistemmed suckering (rhizomatous) woody shrubs to herbaceous, mat-forming plants. They are primarily deciduous, although some evergreen species do exist. Most dogwoods bear opposite leaves. They provide the "D" in the MAD Horse rule—that introductory rule taught to all plant materials students trying to remember the majority of plants with opposite leaves: "M" is for maple, "A" is for ash (including the genus *Fraxinus*, along with all the other members of its family, *Oleaceae*), and "D" is for dogwood. The "horse" refers to all members of the genus *Aesculus*, including the horsechestnut. (There's another useful purpose for that pesky plant taxonomy.) Those who take the rule a step further know it as the MAD Horse Cap rule, "Cap" standing for the family *Caprifoliaceae*, which includes such genera as *Lonicera* and *Viburnum*.

Foliage

Dogwood leaves are typically ovate, simple, and entire along the margin. The lower leaf surface is often covered with copious quantities of single-celled T-shaped trichomes (liquid-filled, hairlike structures) loaded with calcium carbonate. All dogwood leaves show a rather unique arcuate veination, the major veins arranged much like lines of longitude on the globe. In addition, the major leaf veins contain a latexlike substance that forms strands when pulled apart. Thus,

Cornus florida

dogwood leaves make a wonderful magic trick for amusing small children. "Separate" the leaf into two halves and watch the second half rise when you lift the first. Ok, not a very good bar trick, but it does work on *very* young kids.

Most dogwood species sport medium green summer foliage, and with the exception of the many variegated forms, few are standouts in this regard. But it is in autumn that the leaves can really shine. Reds, yellows, oranges, and burgundy shades can develop alone or in concert to form spectacular autumnal dress. To be truthful, on the full family scale, there are as many poor fall-coloring species as there are those that would inspire poets. Dogwoods seem to have benefited from wonderful public relations in this realm.

Flowers

Of course, the flowers are what make the dogwood. Just the mere mention of the name dogwood conjures up images of sprightly spring days of crystal blue skies, fresh morning breezes, and the clear proud glow of a flowering dogwood in bloom. While this does a bit of injustice to the entire clan (by far, most dogwoods don't have flowers that most casual observers would call *dogwood* flowers), for many this is the image of spring. In the eastern and central United States, the Pacific Northwest, throughout much of temperate Asia and parts of Europe, there is probably no better-recognized, -loved, or -planted small flowering tree than *Cornus florida*, the flowering dogwood. There are dogwood festivals, subdivisions, shopping centers, and more. In Kentucky, we even celebrate annually dogwood winter, that late spring cold snap at dogwood bloom time that reminds us all that the tomato plants we just set out can still experience a rude reminder of Mother Nature's occasional mean-spirited jokes. No, there are few who would argue the flowering dogwood's position as top dog among the spring-flowering trees.

Yet, as many learn in grade school, or at least in an introductory plant materials class, the flowers of *Cornus florida* aren't white at all. Of course, the true flowers are yellow to yellow-green and not more than 0.25 inch (6 mm) across. The show is apparent in what are called involucral bracts that subtend the boss of 20 to 30 true flowers. These are the outer protective structures evident in the winter bud that sits at the end of most dormant branches. Still, a sure way to win a quick beer at a spring neighborhood barbeque is to bet the host on the color of his or her dogwood's flowers. It's a winner every time.

All *Cornus* species bear their true flowers in compound inflorescences described as cymose, paniculate, corymbose, umbellate, or capitate. Translated, that means a more-or-less rounded, flat or spherical mass of from as few as 8 to as many as 50 flowers, mostly born at the ends of branches of the previous season's growth. And while there is fair variation in the show provided by the bloom, the individual flowers from all species are quite consistent. Most are four-petaled flowers of creamy white to yellow-green, perfect (dioecious—male and female flowers born on separate plants—in the African species), and almost all are self-sterile. In some species like *C. florida* and *C. kousa* the show of the true flowers is easily overwhelmed by the show of the expanded bracts. Others produce a more pin-cushion-like inflorescence of creamy white with no showy bracts. This is typical in *C. alba*, *C. alternifolia*, and all their kissin' cousins. Still others have followed a different path and accentuated the true flowers with a bright splash of sulfur yellow: *C. mas* and friends. Across the family, flowering time can vary from the February-March gold of *C. mas* to the midsummer show of *C. macrophylla*, nearly six months of flowering from a single small group of plants in the garden.

Fruit

Once the flowering subsides, it is time for the fruit to take center stage. Botanically, the fruit is described as a drupe or drupacaeous berry (any more question as to why science writing as a genre has taken so long to make it onto the best-seller lists?) and can range from white, to yellow, cherry red, and dark bluish black. From a show standpoint, leading the charge once again is *Cornus florida*. Individual bright red, oval fruits up to 0.4 inch (9 mm) long form in groups of up to about 15 or so. They are closely rivaled in showiness by that of *C. canadensis* and its relatives. But all make a splendid show of bright, glossy red fruits nestled into a delightful foil of bright green. They are formed brightly, held proudly, and often taken quickly by foraging birds. Still, some can remain on the plant to extend the show into late autumn. Yellow forms of the normally red-fruited dogwoods result from the absence of two anthocyanins (peonidin and petunidin), pigments typically found in fruit exocarp (skin).

In *Cornus kousa*, the individual football-like fruits, which resemble those of *C. florida*, have fused into a syncarp, a compound structure most closely resembling a large round raspberry. It is almost as if one took the *C. florida* fruit mass down to the local filling station and inflated it with one of those over-powered air hoses.

Cornus florida

Most dogwood species produce fruit of a more somber nature. Creamy white to blue-black is the norm for most of the shrubby species and some of the small trees as well. They are generally produced in flat, rounded arrangements and at best are considered moderately showy. While plant geeks around the planet like to wax eloquent about such modest features, the bottom line is that black is black, and few non-plant enthusiasts consider it showy. How many garden center customers come in on a sunny Saturday morning looking for something with black fruit?

While dogwoods win many pageants in the show category, they are fairly limited in the culinary world. *Cornus mas* is the true one-and-only standout in this category. The bright cherry red fruits, while incredulously tart in early summer, ripen to a range of pleasantly tart to downright sweet. About the best way to know one is harvesting appropriately ripe fruit is to sit beneath a plant with open hands. When a fruit drops into your hands, it is just about ready. Of course, the birds would have been there the day before so you may be standing out there for quite some time. Each fruit does have a large stone and limited pulp, but a bucketful cooked down and strained can produce fabulous jellies, jams, and preserves. Several cultivars from eastern Europe have been selected for large, pulpy fruit and are grown commercially on a limited basis.

Most of the other red-fruited species bear edible but not overly palatable fruit. Historically, *Cornus canadensis* has been used as a minor food crop by some northern North American tribes, but it is not likely to show up in trendy restaurants any time soon. There seem to be no historical references to any food uses of the white-to black-fruited species. In fact, like many plants that civilization has chosen not to domesticate, these have an effect on the human anatomy that might earn them the name "Zumilax."

Bark

Finally, we come to dogwood bark. Many a bored undergraduate eye has rolled at the one comedic entry of the genus. How can you tell a dogwood? By its bark, of course! My (Paul's) 10-year-old has gotten great mileage out of that one. But unlike most bad jokes, this one actually can point us in a reasonable direction.

Cornus stolonifera var. *coloradensis*

Bark texture and coloration not only provide an outstanding identification feature, but also open another whole realm of ornamental usefulness for the genus. It is here that some of the shrubby species, so often relegated to the back row of the choir in terms of flower and fruit show, finally get their due. Where would the winter landscape be without the red, yellow, orange, and coral bark of *Cornus alba*, *C. stolonifera*, and *C. sanguinea*? They provide the seldom-found combination in garden plants of industrial strength with outstanding ornamental appeal. Placed against an evergreen backdrop of *Abies balsamea* (for the northerners), *Picea orientalis*, *Cephalotaxus*, *Buxus*, even the venerable *Taxus*, dogwoods provide a brilliant contrast for the winter-weary gardener. Better still, a light dusting of the winter white stuff over the brilliant-colored stems casts all the makings of calendar and postcard.

Continuing to turn the horticultural tables on the typical front-runners, our old favorites, *Cornus florida* and *C. kousa*, now take up a position back in the pack. Their bark, distinctive as it is, doesn't hold a candle to the bark of *C. alba* and its friends. Bark on a mature *C. florida* is often described as blocky or produced in a jigsaw puzzle pattern. Good for winter ID but not showy.

A few rungs up the bark ladder from *Cornus florida* is *C. kousa*. While not a showstopper from 50 paces, the micro-camouflage patterning of olive, cream, gray, and coppery brown does create a nice, close-up impact in the garden. The fine exfoliation pattern plays beautifully against bold foliage beneath. Think *Rodgersia*, even large blue hostas.

Dogwood Breeding and Selection

As is plainly obvious from the listing in this work, a dizzying volume of attention has been paid to the identification, procurement, and sale of superior forms of many of the *Cornus* species. What likely represents the earliest of this work traces back to classical Greece and Rome where *C. mas* was occasionally referenced as a fruit crop. While not ever reaching the diet staple status of other more common fruits, it was used occasionally for producing a wine of acceptable quality, apparently if one drank enough of it. No ancient references to crop improvement in *C. mas* have survived to the present day; however, considering the attention paid to improved forms of other fruit crops at that time, it would be hard to believe that similar attention was not paid to the cornelian cherry dogwood. If this was the case, the only surviving influence we might hope to find today would be in improved seed strains having maintained some of the selected-for characteristics in wild stands of the species.

With today's clamor for new forms of *Cornus kousa* and related species, one might think we should immediately look to China and Japan for historical volumes on improvement and selection of superior forms. Just look to the tremendous regional efforts of ancient China around such work on *Paeonia*, *Rosa*, *Prunus*, and the like. Although one would expect equal attention paid to the dogwoods, this seems to be mostly absent from the historical record. While *C. kousa* and other members of the clan have been grown in gardens for generations, for some reason the selection work there never quite reached the same level of activity.

In the modern era, we look to the *Cornus alba* and *C. florida* groups to find early evidence of crop improvement. Some of the currently available cultivars of *C. alba* date to the mid and late nineteenth century, and while confident cultivar identity in that group can be quite a mind bender these days, with some focused effort one could tease out these long-standing selections. One need only to look at catalogs from the mid to late nineteenth century of the famed Hess Nursery of Germany, even the various Veitch nurseries of England of the same time, to find listings of *C. alba* 'Sibirica' and 'Hessei'.

Almost immediately following the movement of Europeans into the New World, *Cornus florida* became a hot commodity back home. Enormous quantities of seed were shipped back to primarily England where the emerging seedlings were plagued by a general lack of warmth (the air, not the gardeners). Plants generally found themselves planted along the south face of walls to provide extra warmth to help ripen the wood through the season. Seedlings of *C. florida* were much sought after, and copious quantities of TLC were dished out to keep prized specimens alive no matter how pathetic the specimen. My how our spots have remained unchanged.

Following Marc Catesby's 1731 report of the pink-bracted *Cornus florida*, the variety created a resurgence of interest in the species and we started the whole ball of silliness all over again. Still, large-scale nursery production of selected clones remained a non-issue until about the 1950s.

Records of the first efforts to produce and sell improved *Cornus florida* selections are very sketchy. *Cornus florida* 'Pendula' is listed in an 1880 catalog of Meehan Nursery, Philadelphia, Pennsylvania. Various multibracted forms are listed starting in the late 1800s also. The Arnold Arboretum of Jamaica Plain, Massachusetts, lists a plant of *C. florida* 'Fastigiata' growing in the collections since 1910. Interestingly, *C. florida* 'Ascending' was patented in 1952, just two years before the Arnold Arboretum released 'Fastigiata' to the nursery trade. In 1967 Donald Wyman indicated these two to likely be the same selection. Could this be the first documented case of a patented plant representing a rename of a previously existing cultivar? There are those pesky unchanging spots again. *Cornus florida* 'Xanthocarpa' is listed as of 1919, but there is no indication in the literature if this represents a seed strain or a clone.

In the 1930s things started hopping with selection of several pink forms of *Cornus florida*. Henry Hicks of the famed Hicks Nursery in Long Island, New York, released *C. florida* 'Belmont Pink', a form that seems to have disappeared from the trade. *Cornus florida* 'Wine Red' was selected and named in 1917 and subsequently listed in the 1938 and 1939 catalogs of Howell Nursery, Sweetwater, Tennessee. The selection was very likely renamed 'Prosser Red' some 20 years later.

The first improved white-bracted selections to go into heavy clonal production were *Cornus florida* 'Cherokee Princess', 'Springtime', and 'Hillenmeyer'. As the story goes, Don's father, Hoskins Shadow, started producing large numbers of the three, intent on charging a premium for these budded, improved white forms to match the premium being charged then for budded pink forms. Thinking that nobody in their right mind would pay extra for a "plain old white dogwood," some colleagues of Mr. Shadow anointed him "Crazy Shadow." Given the tens of millions of dollars of sales of these improved forms today, one might just say, "Crazy like a fox."

The most significant recent work with *Cornus florida* has come from the Tennessee Agricultural Experiment Station, which has introduced several selections geared at resistance to powdery mildew. *Cornus florida* 'Jean's Appalachian Snow' and 'Kay's Appalachian Mist' have shown excellent resistance, while 'Karen's Appalachian Blush' has shown some susceptibility.

In the world of *Cornus kousa*, selection and introduction of superior cultivars have been a relatively recent phenomenon. Probably the most significant but most often overlooked bit of work in this species came with Ernest "Chinese" Wilson's 1907 introduction into the United States of the Chinese variety of the species. From this seed collection and subsequent introductions of the variety have come many of our most vigorous, floriferous, and overall drop-dead-gorgeous cultivars. One of the earliest of these is 'China Girl', a Dutch selection introduced around 1910. The Wayside Gardens (of Mentor, Ohio) introduction of the 'Milky Way'

Cornus florida 'Cherokee Princess'

seed strain in the 1960s, while resulting in 35 years of utter confusion in the trade (see cultivar description), did lead to subsequent selection and introduction of some outstanding clones. The 1970s and 1980s saw a burst of activity in white *C. kousa* selections, with the most concentrated efforts coming from Polly Hill and Polly Wakefield, two outstanding New England gardeners. Hill's introductions from her garden on Martha's Vineyard (now the Polly Hill Arboretum) include 'Big Apple', 'Square Dance', and 'Blue Shadow' (her best effort and named for Don). Wakefield's selections seem to have originated primarily from *C. kousa* var. *chinensis* stock and include one of the very best white-bracted forms of *C. kousa* on the market today in 'Greensleeves'.

The first significant work in the pink kousa dogwoods came in the form of the 1970 seed crop from which 17th-generation Japanese nurseryman Toshihiru Hagiwara selected 'Beni Fuji'. The 1980s Japanese selection and introduction of 'Miss Satomi' from Akiri Shibamichi, while now somewhat mixed up in the U.S. trade, made quite a spectacle. Seed of 'Miss Satomi' has produced some exciting new forms now coming available in the United States and beyond.

As impressive as all the above work has been, it has represented a selection of improved forms from Mother Nature's genetic one-armed bandits. Plant a pile of dogwood seed and see what you get. None of the above have resulted from controlled hybridization using specifically chosen parents. In that most dogwoods are self-sterile, what we have been looking at to this point is the result of chance meetings in the night of two horticultural ships. Not that this work should be given short shrift. It takes a keen eye and extensive knowledge of the species in question to be able to recognize a true standout in a field of 100,000 seedlings. As noted plantsman Keith Warren of the J. Frank Schmidt Company puts it,

> Finding the next great plant is a one in a million chance, and since we plant about 10 million seedlings a year, we should have 10 winners from every year's crop. The only problem is that we have to figure out which 10 are the winners.

Large-scale grow-outs of thousands or millions of seedlings is one way to find excellent selections, but it takes a great deal of space and quite an eye indeed.

Controlled breeding in dogwoods seems to be a twentieth-century invention. There is no evidence for any controlled breeding prior to the early 1960s when Elwin Orton, the king of dogwood breeding, began his work. Originally working with *Cornus kousa* and *C. florida* crosses, Orton realized the goals of his 20 years of work with the introduction of the six original hybrids of *C. ×rutgersensis*. Of course, the serendipitous result of this work was that Orton's new introductions hit the market at the height of the dogwood anthracnose appearance and as it turned out, his hybrids, intermediate in characteristics between the two parents, carried *C. kousa*'s high resistance to the *Discula destructiva* fungus. Talk about being in the right place at the right time! But placing credit where credit is due, Orton began his breeding program with full knowledge of the range of ornamental and cultural characteristics in both gene pools. This was no fluke. Orton has continued his program, with the most recent introductions including *C. nuttallii* in two- and three-way crosses. His *C. kousa* × *C. nuttallii* Venus™ may very well be the best yet.

One of the very best and brightest plant breeders to hit the woody ornamentals world in the 1990s has fortunately turned some of his attentions to the genus *Cornus*. Tom Ranney of North Carolina State University has been working with *C. kousa* and several of the related evergreen and semievergreen species. And if his past work with *Calycanthus, Ilex, Hypericum, Stewartia,* and so forth are any indication, a superstar is in the making.

Insect and Disease Problems

By far the most significant pest of the genus *Cornus* is the two-legged, Briggs-and-Stratton-wielding weekend landscape warrior. Take a typically understory species like *C. florida* that thrives in the partly shady wood with nice rich organic soils all moist and acidic. Once the plant leaves the nursery for that long trunk ride to its new home, the game is just about over. Despite all encouragement and direction, most homeowners run right home and find the sunniest, driest, and nastiest site with the poorest excuse for soil available to them.

Now to be fair, most homeowners are not left much in the way of soil around their new houses. Some gardeners out there will buy a house or not move based on the quality of their garden soil. They are out there. We all know at least one. But most people are not that crazy, so they drop these poor unsuspecting specimens into their clay tombs for a short walk down an even shorter plank. Then, while the poor plant is suffering its newest insult, out of the garage comes the 10,000-horsepower, internal combustion, riding death machine. It may only be a quarter acre (one-tenth hectare) of lawn but by golly, that four-wheel drive unit with the 48-inch (120-cm) cut is essential. It runs screaming along, cutting, blowing, mulching, and sucking up everything in its path and doing a generally marvelous job until the inevitable problem arises; the operator has to turn around the death machine without hitting the house or the new minivan, or running out over the curb. "If I can just cut it a little tighter I just might be able to . . . "—whack! Right into the side of the little struggling dogwood, stripping off half the bark about 3 inches (7.5 cm) above the ground.

Amazingly, this major infraction of gardening etiquette seems to almost energize the plant. Rather than taking a graceful swan dive toward its future existence as mulch for other trees, this treatment seems to make the tree just hang on for several years in a sort of suspended and rather straggly animation. A sad sight and no way to treat one of our greatest natural treasures. Yes, although one rarely sees this listed in plant pathology text books, the most significant malady of the small tree dogwoods is none other than mower blight.

But seriously, most dogwoods are reasonably tolerant species if given appropriate siting and even minimum care. Generally, most will thrive in just about any slightly acidic average garden soil that is supplemented with a bit of moisture through the driest parts of the summer.

Stem Canker

In the shrub dogwoods, *Cornus alba* and most of its bright barked relatives, the most serious disease problem is stem canker. The malady causes dieback of the cambium layer just below the outer bark and is easily spotted as a dark sunken lesion, usually located close to the ground level. If plants are coppiced annually or thereabouts, canker is rarely a problem. Likewise, plants grown on evenly moist soils with good drainage show far less canker than those planted with wet feet. Truth be known, plants of *C. alba* and *C. stolonifera* planted in heavy, wet, and soggy soil will likely fade from root rot before they have a chance to die from canker. Canker is not nearly as significant a problem in the less showy barked species such as *C. racemosa*.

Canker can also be a significant problem on *Cornus alternifolia*. Here the problem seems less to do with site conditions and more to do with the constant pull and tug between host and pathogen. Plants can sail along perfectly happily with all kinds of vigor and looking just fine and then one spring, a large limb will fail to leaf out. Close inspection where the live and dead stem sections come together usually reveals a small canker that has progressed all the way around the stem thus cutting off the plumbing to the affected limb. This seems to affect healthy as well as stressed plants, and while not serious enough a problem to limit use of the species, it can be occasionally frustrating.

For control of dogwood canker, the gardener can only look to cultural techniques. No chemical controls are available. Plants should be kept vigorous and free from stress, but not overfertilized. As with many pathogen problems, plants showing extremely vigorous and succulent growth are much more susceptible. With the bright barked shrub types, the best control may be to coppice, or annually prune to the ground in late winter. Canker shows up most often on older branches.

Dogwood Anthracnose

The designer pathogen since 1970 has been so-called dogwood anthracnose caused by the fungus *Discula destructiva*, and destructive it is. This pathogen was unknown to science prior to the mid 1970s and, since its appearance, it has spread rapidly through native populations. A 1978 report on the dogwood populations of Connecticut and New York described a dieback ailment that was subsequently identified as belonging to the genus *Discula* in 1983. By 1987, it was identified in Delaware, Maryland, Massachusetts, New Jersey, New York, Pennsylvania, Virginia, and West Virginia. The range of disease on native flowering dogwoods now spans from Vermont to Georgia and west to Tennessee, Kentucky, Michigan, and Missouri.

On the West Coast, a similar ailment was described in Washington State in 1979 and by 1983 was identified as the same organism as that causing disease in the East. In the four years between its discovery and identification in Washington, the disease had spread to Idaho, Oregon, and British Columbia. Based on the rapid spread and other characteristics of the progression of the disease, *Discula destructiva* is believed by many plant pathologists to be an introduced pathogen. Mysteriously, the source of the organism is unknown and has not been identified as occurring naturally anywhere outside North America. However unknown as it may be, the pathogen has wreaked havoc on native populations of *Cornus florida* in the East and *C. nuttallii* in the West.

Dogwood anthracnose has had its most significant impact on native populations, especially in moist wooded climates. In the southeastern United States, the spread has been quickest and the impact most severe in mountainous areas where cloud fog is prevalent during the key infection period. A 1986 report listed the results of a survey of the native population of *Cornus florida* of the Catoctin Mountain National Park in Maryland. According to this report, 3 percent of the plants surveyed in 1984 showed no signs of anthracnose and 33 percent were dead. A follow-up report indicated that in the same population four years later all trees were infected, 89 percent were dead, and there appeared to be no regeneration of young plants. Ironically, from this decimated population comes the first *C. florida* cultivar selected specifically for resistance to dogwood anthracnose. 'Appalachian Spring' was one of the few plants to survive the devastating impact of the disease organism and is being released by the Tennessee Agricultural Experiment Station. The Brooklyn Botanic Garden also reports working with several potentially resistant plants from the Mohonk Preserve in New Paltz, New York.

Dogwood anthracnose seems to require moist springs and falls to do its worst but is aided by stress brought on by drought and winter injury to host plants. In *Cornus florida*, the disease begins with irregular leaf or bract lesions, 0.25 inch (6 mm) in diameter, that are tan or brown in the center, surrounded by purplish rims. Leaves can also show marginal and vein necrosis, and as the season progresses, spots may coalesce to form large lesions. If the disease progresses, the pathogen will proceed through the leaf, working down through the petiole and eventually to the young twigs and all the way to the main trunk. Plants so affected often hold onto the dead brown leaves for a sure telltale sign of dogwood anthracnose. Once the disease enters the young shoot, stem lesions form, initially at the leaf nodes, and eventually girdle the stem causing twig dieback. In severe and successive infections, the heavy twig dieback is followed by loss of major limbs in the lower part of the crown and sprouting of epicormic shoots. These soft vigorous shoots are extremely susceptible to re-infection and at this point the tree is a goner.

In *Cornus nuttallii* the infection can be similar but can also begin as fall leaf blight resulting in death of the terminal bud and then in following growing seasons, the typical sprouting and re-infection. In large trees of both species (*C. florida* and *C. nuttallii*), initial infection to loss of the entire tree is typically a multiyear process, but heavily infected trees rarely last more than three or four years. Young infected seedlings may die the same year. In the landscape where disease pressure is not as strong, gardeners would do best to mulch lightly, use drip irrigation in the dry part of the summer, avoid overfertilization, and clean up leaves in the fall.

The surface of stem lesions and the lower surface of leaf spots develop reproductive structures that produce enormous quantities of spores and lead to disease spread. The best control measures are to maintain plant vigor and health through maintenance of adequate soil moisture, fertility, and good sanitation. Avoid overfertilization since the resultant soft growth is highly susceptible to infection. Also avoid overhead irrigation since this can spread the spores by splashing and also leaves water droplets on the foliage, a requirement for spore germination.

While dogwood anthracnose is primarily known as a disease of *Cornus florida* and *C. nuttallii*, some infections on *C. kousa* have been reported but few serious outbreaks. Symptoms on *C. kousa* typically remain as foliar lesions and do not progress to the more severe stages.

Spot Anthracnose

Not to be confused with dogwood anthracnose, spot anthracnose caused by the organism *Elsinoe corni*, is primarily a disease with more aesthetic impact than anything else. While very heavy infestations may inhibit buds from opening, they rarely kill plants by themselves.

Spring occurrences of spot anthracnose can resemble an early outbreak of *Discula destructiva*. Spots may appear first on the bracts (more often on whites than pinks) and later on the emerging leaves. This affliction, however, is easy to distinguish from dogwood anthracnose in that spot anthracnose lesions are small, 0.12–0.25 inch (3–6 mm) in diameter, light brown to white in the center, and spread uniformly on the surface. Later in the season, the center may fall out of the foliar lesions leaving shot holes on puckered leaves. Occasionally, spots may form on young twigs and fruit, but the disease progression stops there.

The causal organism generally overwinters on the tree rather than in fallen leaves. Twigs, stems, and retained leaves and fruit are its typical winter homes. Spot anthracnose is generally a problem in cool moist springs. Treatment is generally not recommended; however, fungicide sprays through the bloom period and continuing for several weeks following flowering can be effective. Late summer sprays can also help to reduce the severity of the disease symptoms the following spring.

Septoria Leaf Spot

The last of the major leaf spot problems is *Septoria* leaf spot caused by *Septoria cornicola*. This foliar insult occurs primarily in late summer or fall and is little cause for concern. In this case, the spots are 0.25 inch (6 mm) in diameter and dark brown, angular in outline, and tend not to cross veins. Again, the spot margin may be a deep purple tone. Generally, this disease is a vanity issue. Chemical controls can be used, but it is usually best, and most responsible, to simply practice good garden sanitation. In that the organism overwinters in fallen leaves, a good raking and compost pile should do the trick nicely.

Powdery Mildew

Beyond the leaf spots, a foliar problem that has in recent years become about as serious as any other dogwood disease is powdery mildew. Powdery mildew is a generic label applied variously to a wide range of foliar fungi of ornamental plants. Why what would the late summer boarder be without a nice bright silver *Monarda* or *Phlox* covered in mildew? But in *Cornus*, this was not a problem up until the 1990s. In some parts of the United States, this is now considered the primary disease problem in *C. florida*.

Powdery mildew in dogwoods is caused primarily by *Microsphaeria pennicillata* (synonym *M. pulchra*) and *Phyllactinia guttata*. It typically infects plants in springs offering warm days and cool nights with humid air. Oddly enough, frequent rain may lessen disease pressure. Spores are released primarily from old leaves on the ground and are spread through air currents. Spring symptoms show up as a faint white almost bloomy coating to stems, buds, and leaves. As the summer progresses, leaves will show brown patches, puckering, and some reddening. As the symptoms advance, plants look moisture stressed. While isolated and occasional disease problems may just set plants back a bit, repeated infection can seriously drain trees and predispose them to secondary pathogens.

Control of powdery mildew can be accomplished with several fungicides; however, future dogwoods will likely run with resistance genes that show up prominently in trials. The disease is most significant in *Cornus florida*, but will also show up in *C. kousa, C. nuttallii*, and to a lesser extent in some of the shrub species. As mentioned elsewhere in this text, the Tennessee Agricultural Experiment Station has released three promising *C. florida* cultivars: 'Jean's Appalachian Snow', 'Karen's Appalachian Blush', and 'Kay's Appalachian Mist'. Among the pink-bracted flowering dogwoods, 'Cherokee Brave' and 'Sweetwater Red' have been the most resistant. The *C. ×rutgersensis* hybrids show fairly good resistance to powdery mildew.

Dogwood Borer

One of the primary insect problems of dogwoods is plain old dogwood borer. While there are more than half a dozen borer type insects that can infect the members of the genus *Cornus*, it is the dogwood borer, *Synanthedon scitula*, that can have the greatest impact on primarily the tree-form dogwoods.

We start the story of a dogwood borer with the adult. Mature insects are 0.5 inch (12 mm) long, with a blue-black body sporting yellow racing stripes and clear wings. As the bracts on *Cornus florida* drop in spring, the adult insects take to the air and deposit eggs along the main trunk and branches. They are especially fond of bark openings, fresh pruning cuts, and any type of mechanical damage to the bark. (This, of course, is where mower blight can have such a big impact.) The larvae are white grubs with a brown head and are 0.5 inch (12 mm) long. They will feed under the bark, overwinter there, feed again a bit in the spring, and then emerge.

Dogwood borer symptoms are hard to miss: exit wounds 0.12 inch (3 mm) in diameter will yield coarse sawdust and the surrounding area will look like there are lumpy mashed potatoes under the bark. Eventually the bark will slough off and at this point, one should have the chipper well oiled and warmed up. Some gardeners will employ Herculean efforts to bring half-dead specimens back to life, but it is simply not worth the effort in most cases.

As with most dogwood problems, this pest is most significant on stressed or mechanically damaged trees. Gardeners should keep trees well irrigated, appropriately fertilized, and in generally good condition. It is also advisable to avoid pruning in late spring as the fresh pruning wounds seem to just ring the dinner bell for the hovering moths. Trunk sprays during *Cornus florida* bloom time can be effective at controlling the insects.

CHAPTER 2

THE
Cornus canadensis
GROUP

Cornus canadensis belongs to a minor group of species and naturally occurring hybrids that seem to give taxonomists and gardeners fits. For taxonomists, the group may be typically overpassed, but for the successful gardener, it consists of plants worth the effort of growing. The group includes dogwoods that choose to exist as herbaceous or suffruticose plants, mostly consisting of ephemeral aerial shoots arising from woody and fleshy rhizome systems. The two species, *C. canadensis* and *C. suecica*, hybridize freely where their ranges overlap, to give rise to *C. ×unalaschkensis*. Gotta love that name!

Cornus canadensis
BUNCHBERRY, BEAR BERRY, BEAR GRAPE, KINNIKINICK

Cornus canadensis forms a low mat of dense foliage to 10 inches (25 cm) high and can spread in broad colonies. In the eastern barrens of Maine, where the species is actually a weed in commercial blueberry fields, individual plants of bunchberry can spread more than 10 to 15 feet (3–4.5 m) across. Imagine that if you are a frustrated gardener who has struggled to keep your 12-inch (30-cm) square plant from becoming a single stem specimen.

The plant produces opposite pairs of leaves ranging widely in size from 0.5 to 2.5 inches (12–65 mm) long. They are short-petioled, 0.25–0.5 inch (6–12 mm) long, with more pinnate veination than is typical of related plants. The leaves are broadly elliptical and acute at both ends. Foliage color is a flat green, changing to deep burgundy in the fall. The fall color may sound appealing but in a mulched garden bed, the autumnal foliage seems to blend into the mulch and plants almost disappear from view.

The true flowers are creamy white to occasionally pink, in short umbels up to 0.75 inch (2 cm) across. They are nestled snugly into two tightly spaced pairs of what look to be perfect miniature *Cornus florida* bracts. The bracts are acute at both ends, slightly recurved in some plants, and creamy white. The entire floral display can extend up to about the diameter of a golf ball or just slightly more—an unwelcome characteristic for those who try to practice their golf and gardening in the same woods. Flowers emerge in late May to June in Maine.

Occasionally, one hears excited reports of a pink-bracted *Cornus canadensis*. We all (*Cornus* geeks, that is) scramble around, positioning and dealing, to obtain this botanical holy grail. Of course, what we know will inevitably be the case. The pink turns out to be a simple manifestation of moisture stress. As of this writing, when it comes to pink bunchberry, it is still buyer beware!

In their native haunts, these procumbent species mix with mosses, lichens,

Cornus canadensis

low species of *Vaccinium* (blueberries), *Arctostaphylos*, and *Gaultheria*—excellent company indeed. The combination of a flowering mat of *Cornus canadensis* in concert with pink-blushed *Vaccinium angustifolum* flowers and the deep glossy green of *Gaultheria* foliage is a picture worthy of Monet's brush. For now, photographic emulsion will have to suffice.

Following the flowers, small round clusters of cherry-red fruits form, nestled nicely into the bright green summer foliage. The fruit will ripen in midsummer and may stay effective through early fall. They are typically eaten by birds and small foraging mammals. Once all the spring wildflowers have faded from view, bunchberry fruit is one of the few bright spots of color on the summer woodland floor. Some dogwood enthusiasts (admittedly few) have worked on taking the sprightly fruit one step further. Work in Europe has focused on *Cornus canadensis* production as a Christmas season potted plant. The bright green foliage holds up quite well, and with the woodland foragers gone, the fruit can last for several months in the right conditions. It has not yet shown up on the post-Thanksgiving Wal-Mart display tables, but one never knows.

One of the reasons Maine and Canadian blueberry growers spray Roundup™ on bunchberry growing in their fields, beside the fact that the latter occupies valuable acreage in the field, is that the bunchberry fruits can become a contaminant of the harvested blueberries. They are easily separated, however, as bunchberry fruits float and blueberries typically sink. Fruit of the two *Cornus* species and their hybrid are indistinguishable.

Cornus canadensis

Culture of bunchberry is one of those enigmas of the gardening world. The plant grows naturally in the most inhospitable and variable places: USDA hardiness zone 2 or 3, in soggy bogs; in full sun on sandy eskers of eastern Maine; and in the deep, dense shade of spruce and pine woods of the north country and south through the higher elevation Appalachians. Surely with that diversity, the plant should be adaptable to a wide range of garden conditions. Alas, once again, Mother Nature has thrown us a knuckleball. As it turns out, outside its natural range, the plant is an absolute beast to grow.

Most of the cultural problems with bunchberry seem to stem from its seeming intolerance of warm temperatures, especially warm night and soil temperatures. As one tries to drag the plant kicking and screaming south, the first thing that goes is the flowering. Some folks can grow a nice crop of foliage but get little in the way of flowers. And as much as we might adore the plant, without the flowers, bracts, and fruit, it is just another leafy weed in the garden. With most of us having more favorite plants than garden space, a non-flowering bunchberry is just too high a price to pay.

Moving still farther south, the plant actually does an amazing shrinking act. Plant a mat of, say, 50 stems in the spring and by July 4th those 50 will be down to 35. By season's end, the lucky gardener will still have 8 or 10. For those southern gardeners wishing to have a lush carpet of bunchberry in their gardens, the best advice is to move north or at least up high in the mountains. As far south as the Carolinas, one can find beautiful populations of the species, but only at the higher elevations.

Other than thermal crankiness, the species demonstrates an absolute requirement for acid soils. Indeed, in some of its native haunts, the natural soil pH can be as low as 4.0. There's not enough sulfur on the planet to get Paul's Kentucky soil with a pH of 7.1 down to 4.0 and keep it there easily.

Assuming one resides, or at least gardens in the northern zones, propagation is quite easy. Seed propagation requires harvest of fresh fruit and immediate removal of the pulp. This can be accomplished painstakingly slowly by rubbing fruit on a screen. A simpler procedure is to mix about half a cup (one-tenth liter) of fruit in about two cups (half a liter) of water in a blender. A few pulses of the motor can save ounces of finger skin from the torture of the screen. The blender process will result in some seeds being destroyed, but it is by far the best way to go. To make the process a little easier, soak the fruit in a bucket of water overnight to soften the pulp.

Seed of *Cornus canadensis* requires scarification prior to stratification to allow for water absorption. This can be accomplished fairly easily with a 60-minute soak in concentrated sulfuric acid and should be done with the treatment vessel sitting in an ice bath to reduce temperature build-up. Of course, not everyone has 12-molar sulfuric acid sitting in the pantry. In the Cappiello household, Paul finds it is hard enough to keep his wife from "cleaning out" the refrigerator and throwing away all his seeds. So for those with equally unsympathetic (or worse, less sympathetic), non-gardening refrigerator partners, skip the acid and go for the blender. Turns out, the blender cleaning treatment does a fairly nice job of scarifying a good portion of the seeds. Sure, you lose a few seeds in the process but the cleaning is faster and you don't have to install an OSHA-approved fume hood in your house to deal with the sulfuric acid fumes.

Following harvest, cleaning, and scarification, the seeds require about 90 to 120 days of cold, moist stratification. A plastic sandwich zipper bag with a little barely damp sphagnum moss does the trick nicely. The longer the stratification, the more uniform the germination.

Provenance, or the geographical source of the seed, may play an important role in the demonstrated adaptability of the species under cultivation. While in Maine, Paul heard many reports from growers and garden center owners who would buy plants from wholesalers but could not get them to overwinter during a typical New England winter. Being the inquisitive type, Paul did a little searching. What he found was that most wholesale crops of *Cornus canadensis* being brought into New England at the time were produced in the Pacific Northwest. Further, the seed used to produce the plants most often came from sources along the western slopes of the Cascades or similar areas. These locales were typically located in USDA hardiness zones 6 and 7, and possibly more importantly, receive piles upon piles of snow. Therefore, the plants evolved in and adapted to a climate where they rarely see the excruciatingly cold temperatures of a Maine winter. It could be quite simply that the western form may not be as cold hardy as others. Just another in the long list of research projects that would seem to spell job security for horticultural researchers.

Softwood cuttings under intermittent mist root quite readily if treated with 3000 to 5000 ppm K-IBA (the water-soluble potassium—indole butyric acid). Access to a fog system greatly enhances the speed of rooting and the quality of the plants produced. As an alternate propagation method, established rhizome mats may be divided with a spade or cut apart bare-root during the dormant season. One thing to avoid as much as possible is overhead irrigation. In nursery production, too much overhead irrigation leads to very poor foliage quality. In one study conducted at the University of Maine, subsurface irrigation produced fabulous plants, while plants produced under sprinklers looked more like something the cat dragged in. With careful attention though, nice plants can be produced quite rapidly. Softwood cuttings taken from greenhouse-forced plants in March can produce a nicely finished quart-size (liter-sized) plant by the end of the summer.

Cornus canadensis is native from Alaska, south to the mid latitudes of the Rockies, east to Atlantic Canada, New England, and the higher elevations of the Appalachian Mountains. It then picks up again in the mountainous northern portion of Japan. Linnaeus described its distribution as circumboreal and the distribution of *Cornus suecica* as circumpolar.

Like the other members of its group, *Cornus canadensis* is a most beautiful but diminutive dainty plant. Several folks have suggested that *C. canadensis*, *C. suecica*, and *C. ×unalaschkensis* be moved into their own taxonomic domain under the genus *Chamaepericlymenum*. Talk about a mouthful. No wonder most folks are petrified and bewildered by the vagaries of botany. This nomenclatural proposal has been based on the unique explosive nature of the pollen-producing structures of the flowers. True, this oddly, almost science-fiction attack-of-the-mutant-pollen feature is unique among the *Cornaceae*; however, using this one feature to reclassify these dogwoods is akin to Paul's ascribing his wife to a genus other than *Homo* based on her ability to detect his pulling on mismatched socks in the morning without her having to fully awaken. Suffice to say, he'll keep them where they are for now, thank you very much.

Cornus canadensis 'Downeaster' was selected by Paul from the blueberry barrens of eastern Maine where the species grows in full sun, on gravely soils. After five years of evaluation, this selection emerged as the best of the 30 clones tested. It has performed well in gardens as far south as coastal Virginia.

Cornus canadensis, 'Downeaster' (below and below right)

Cornus suecica

Cornus suecica is, as described earlier in this chapter, a close cousin to *C. canadensis*. Its primary visible difference is the gray to purplish true flowers and the foliage more crowded at the tip of each branch. The leaves of *C. suecica* are sessile and show the arcuate veination more typical of the rest of the genus. The species is found along a disjunct circumpolar distribution from northern Europe and the northern British Isles, Greenland, eastern Canada, northeast and northwestern United States, Yukon, Alaska, across to the Aleutian Islands and eastern Russia. Of the two species in its group, *C. suecica* seems to show the more northern tendencies.

One report of *Cornus suecica* in the British Isles indicated that its southern distribution limit corresponds with the 73°F (23°C) isotherm and that within that range plants are only found in areas experiencing greater than about 40 inches (1 m) of annual precipitation. The plant literally pines for the cool moist weather of the north. In addition, *C. suecica* is a distinct calcifuge, growing only in areas with just enough calcium available in the soil and with a typical soil pH of below 5.0. Just what the world needs—a plant more finicky than *C. canadensis*!

Oddly, of all the *Cornus* species, *C. suecica* is the most tolerant of heavy metal content soils and atmospheric sulfur dioxide (SO_2), a significant component of air pollution. Not that air pollution is a significant problem in the Yukon, but nice to know the tolerance is there. Seed of *C. suecica* requires no scarification or cold stratification unlike seed of *C. canadensis*.

Cornus ×unalaschkensis

Leaves of the hybrid *Cornus ×unalaschkensis* tend to be intermediate in veination, not as pinnate as leaves of *C. canadensis* but not as arcuate as leaves of *C. suecica*. Flowers are somewhere in between the creamy white of *C. canadensis* and the dark gray or purple of *C. suecica*. The fruit, however, is indistinguishable from either species.

A final note on *Cornus canadensis* hybrids. Paul has tried on several occasions to cross *C. florida* and *C. canadensis* with no luck at all. From a conversation with Elwin Orton (of *C. florida* × *C. kousa* fame) of Rutgers University, it is apparent that his brief attempts bore no fruit either. Still, Paul's attempts used *C. canadensis* as the female parent but never the other way around. Perhaps there are still possibilities.

Cornus stolonifera 'Garden Glow'

CHAPTER 3

THE
Cornus alba
GROUP

THIS SERVICEABLE GROUP OF DOGWOODS is typified by multistemmed, suckering shrubs, often grown for bright winter bark color. Botanical purists describe the flowers as being born in flat corymbose panicles without involucral bracts. Translation: flat pincushion floral displays without the large showy bracts of *Cornus florida* or *C. kousa*. This group includes some 45 species (depending on whether you are a taxonomic splitter or a lumper).

In this group, one will find the bright red- and yellow-stemmed forms that are so essential to the northern winter garden. In areas were the winter landscape is devoid of the winter-blooming camellias, the January blooms of *Prunus mume*, and myriad other brighteners of the grayest months, these bright shrubby dogwoods are indispensable. Particularly the northern tier of states in the United States—New England, the Midwest, and the north central states—would be considerably poorer without the brilliant colors of the best of this group.

But buyer beware. Most of the rest of the group beyond the bright-stemmed forms could fit under the very generalized description of multistemmed woody shrubs from 6 to 15 feet (1.8–4.5 m) tall with brown, gray, or muted red-brown stems; opposite ovate leaves 1.5–3.5 inches (4–9 cm) long of medium green in summer, turning to a weak yellow to red or falling green; terminal inflorescences from 1.5 to 3 inches (4–7.5 cm) in diameter with individual flowers of cream white; fruit up to 0.25 inch (6 mm) in diameter maturing white to dark blue-black. We haven't set the world on fire here, have we? And neither do the plants. As the short description indicates, these are rather nondescript species. There are subtle differences in morphology, geography, and so forth, but the species are all quite similar. Now certainly this is where the hate mail will come from. Might we now have insulted the International *Cornus rotundifolia* Society with this somewhat flippant treatment of their namesake? However, looking at it from another angle, you just memorized the description of most of the members of this group. Not a bad tradeoff.

With the members of this group of dogwoods, it is the youngest and most vigorous stems or canes that provide the best winter show. Older canes should be removed at the base every winter. Some gardeners prefer to coppice annually, or cut all stems back to the ground. On healthy, established plants, this can produce tremendous growth the following year and an outstanding color display.

Cornus alba, C. stolonifera, and *C. sanguinea* are by far the most commonly planted species in this group and generally the species with the showiest bark, but the list is tremendous. Within the genus *Cornus,* this is by far the largest group in quantity of species and breadth of native range. They cover most of North America, Europe, northern and central Asia, North Africa, and even northern South America.

From a Linnean point of view, a young plant taxonomist looking for recognition (good or bad) in the field could propose lumping many of these species into just a few distinct species with many varieties. The ensuing molecular genetics studies and associated publications could earn tenure for a whole stable of new assistant professors. Of course, the implication here is that the taxonomy is, at best, a mess.

As Paul travels around the United States attending meetings, lecturing, photographing, and otherwise looking busy, he always tries to hook up with those considered experts in the local flora. Why try to teach one's self when individuals out there have spent a lifetime learning the local plants? Almost invariably, as he walks the woods and fields with these individuals, they will come upon one of the ubiquitous and relatively nondescript "shrub dogwoods." Paul savors such instances. Studying from afar the subtle morphological differences in a confusing group such as these plants can drive a plant geek mad. So it is with much anticipation that he ask the obvious question, "Which one is it?" Now mind you, Paul is usually asking the question because he is not as familiar with the local flora as is his host. His host is the considered expert in these here parts. And more importantly, Paul is on a deadline and needs to get these straightened out before the manuscript is due. One can imagine his anticipation. Yet without exception, the response is almost verbatim, "Oh, it's just one of those shrub dogwoods." About the only variation in response involves one or more of various expletives preceding the "shrub dogwoods." Now it is at this point that Paul tries his best to not seem ungrateful. After all, this is the same person who just ten minutes previous was waxing eloquently about the elegant and subtle (invisible?) distinguishing features of two seemingly identical liverworts! "Just one of those shrubby dogwoods" is the best you can do? Seems even the experts have thrown in the towel. Maybe they've never picked up the towel in the first place.

So what's a gardener to do? You might say, "I just want the best red-stemmed form for my garden. It's a nice little spot in front of my garage with a nice dark green *Thuja* hedge in the background. It's not that I don't care about the taxonomy (actually maybe I don't care) but I don't want to have to earn a PhD in molecular biology just to figure out which plant to buy." Well, gardeners, take heart. Those looking for particular characteristics simply need look for specific cultivars based on the descriptions below. Then all that is required is the confidence that the nursery has them labeled correctly. Tread lightly.

Cornus alba
TATARIAN DOGWOOD

Cornus alba carries a description that requires only a subtle edit of the generalized description at the beginning of this chapter. A multi-stemmed suckering shrub 6–10 feet (1.8–3 m) tall and 5–8 feet (1.5–2.4 m) wide, this species tends to be quite upright in branching in youth, with older plants showing some arching tendencies. It differs from the very popular *C. stolonifera* in growth habit in that *C. alba* does not spread by suckers to form large broad colonies as does *C. stolonifera*. In addition, *C. stolonifera* tops out as a mass 4–6 feet (1.2–1.8 m) tall with lax, drooping branches.

The leaves of *Cornus alba* are 2–4 inches (5–10 cm) long, opposite, elliptic to ovate, with an acuminate to acute apex and rounded base. Reddish purple fall color can be attractive if the foliage makes it through the summer in good condition; however, the leaves are often a bit tattered by the time autumn rolls around.

Cornus alba

Numerous variegated and gold-foliaged forms are available. Some make excellent garden specimens; however, they need to be sited with care in some climates. In areas with hot summers and intense sun, the variegation can burn in a very nasty way. Partial shade is quite welcome in these areas. In addition, many of these cultivars show fairly heavy susceptibility to spot anthracnose which can render the foliage quite putrid by midsummer. This malady seems to be far less problematic in the Pacific Northwest. In the eastern, midwestern, and southern United States, it can be downright scary. Good garden sanitation is the gardener's only reasonable weapon in this regard. Variation in cultivar susceptibility is noted in the cultivar descriptions.

Flowers are creamy white, 0.25–0.4 inch (6–9 mm) in diameter, borne in flat-topped cymes, 1.5–3 inches (4–7.5 cm) across, occurring in late May or early June after the leaves have emerged. Of course, the creamy flowers are immediately lost amid the foliage of those cultivars with variegated foliage, but the lasting impact of the foliage generally more than makes amends. Fruit are white to bluish, the brighter colors somewhat showy in years where plants show good red fall foliage. The stone within each fruit is oblong and flattened at the ends. This provides a good distinguishing characteristic from *Cornus stolonifera*, the stone of which is not flattened at the ends.

Brilliant red winter stem color is the primary reason to grow *Cornus alba*. The color is variable over the year, most forms showing greenish red to green-brown in the summer. The bright red color seems to develop in perfect concert with the senescing leaves. Stems can go from dull green to bright coral red in a matter of two weeks. And the more sun on the stems, the brighter the color. Of course, as with all its cousins, the stem color of *C. alba* is always best on young stems from one to three years old. With time, even the most brazen form will show older stems of gray-brown. This is one case where old age does not bring distinguished character.

Young stems bear noticeable white or gray lenticels, the quantity of which can vary from almost lacking to so numerous the stems look like red pretzel rods. Stem pith is white.

The native range of *Cornus alba* is large, spanning from Siberia to the Korean peninsula. The species is fully cold hardy to at least USDA hardiness zone 3. Unbelievably, in laboratory experiments, stems of *C. alba* have survived immersion in liquid nitrogen at almost −392°F (−200°C)! How's that for cold hardy? In the southern states, below about zone 7, the species suffers and is best left off the gardener's palette.

Seed propagation requires 60–90 days of cold, moist stratification of cleaned seed. Stem cuttings root just about any time of year. Softwood cuttings treated with 1000 to 3000 ppm IBA root in just a couple of weeks. Hardwood cuttings treated with 3000 ppm IBA will also root near 100 percent and are sometimes planted directly into field plots. Most of the related members of this group can be propagated in similar fashion with variations listed with the species.

***Cornus alba* 'Albovariegata'** is listed in the *RHS Plant Finder* with the note that it is not found in the literature. This is likely one of the many synonyms for 'Argenteo-marginata'.

***Cornus alba* 'Allemen's Compact'** grows 5 feet (1.5 m) tall and has shorter internodes compared to most of the other cultivars of this species. Winter stems are a muted red and, like most of the red stems, take on more of a green-red mixture in summer. This cultivar is more resistant to leaf spot than many others.

***Cornus alba* 'Argenteo-marginata'** grows 6–8 feet (1.8–2.4 m) tall and is a beautiful form in the summer garden. White-margined leaves have a gray-green center and are moderately susceptible to leaf spot. Stems are dark red in winter and more green than red in summer. The summer foliage is certainly the primary attraction here. Occasional shoots are produced with no chlorophyll in the leaves and brilliantly colored pink-scarlet winter stems. These are an obvious drain on the mother plant and should be removed. This cultivar is an excellent selection for brightening a dark spot in the garden. It is often listed incorrectly as *C. elegantissima* or *C. alba* 'Elegantissima'.

Cornus alba 'Argenteo-marginata'

***Cornus alba* 'Atrosanguinea'** is a dwarf form with bright red stems. It is not often seen in commerce.

***Cornus alba* 'Aurea'** is a surprisingly vigorous form with soft (some might call weak), yellow to chartreuse leaves. In cool summers with even moisture (that is, no moisture

Cornus alba 'Argenteo-marginata'

stress), the foliage stays in excellent condition until autumn. In warmer climes, the leaves show some leaf spot and pigment bleaching. This cultivar is best used in an area with some afternoon shade, especially in southern and midwestern gardens. Essentially all the variegated forms are much happier in the Pacific Northwest. This one produces reasonably good red stems in winter.

***Cornus alba* 'Bailhalo'** (Ivory Halo™), a somewhat compact and fine-stemmed selection, grows 5–6 feet (1.5–1.8 m) tall and wide. The stem color in both winter and summer is not overwhelming, but the weary-eyed winter gardener might call it interesting. This cultivar is moderately susceptible to summer leaf spot. It was discovered in 1983 in a block of *C. alba* 'Argenteo-marginata' by Rod Bailey of Bailey Nurseries, St. Paul, Minnesota. Plant patent number PP8,722.

***Cornus alba* 'Behnschii'** is a moderate-sized selection with variegated leaves of green, white, and dark pink (red). It is highly susceptible to summer leaf spot and can scorch badly in full, hot sun. According to Krüssman (1984), this cultivar originated in the nursery of R. Behnsch, in Duerrgoy near what is now Wroclaw, Poland, before 1898.

Cornus alba **'Bloodgood'** is a selection from the garden of Tom Krenitsky in Chapel Hill, North Carolina. According to the late J. C. Raulston (pers. comm.), this selection had the best winter stem color of any form of *C. alba* in the North Carolina State University Arboretum (now JC Raulston Arboretum) in Raleigh. In piedmont North Carolina tests, 'Bloodgood' proved to be less vigorous in growth than *C. stolonifera* 'Cardinal'.

Cornus alba **'Chblzam'** (Chief Bloodgood™), introduced by Lake County Nursery in Ohio, is described as growing 6 feet (1.8 m) tall and 4–5 feet (1.2–1.5 m) wide. It has brilliant coral-red winter stems, blue fruit, and glossy dark green leaves.

Cornus alba **'Cream Cracker'**, a branch sport of *C. alba* 'Gouchaultii', has gray-green leaf centers surrounded by white margins. It appears to be a weak grower and has shown considerable marginal scorch in Kentucky plantings. This dogwood was discovered by John Pannebakken, Hazerswoude, Netherlands. Plant patent number PP12,830.

Cornus alba 'Cream Cracker'

Cornus alba **'Crimizam'** (Creme de Mint™) is a variegated form with gray-green centers and creamy white margins. The stems are yellow-green. The plant is described as growing to 4.5 feet (1.4 m) tall and wide. It was introduced by Lake County Nursery in Ohio.

Cornus alba **'Gouchaultii'** has a rather wild mixture of yellow-white margins with green, yellow, and pink (red) centers. It makes a unique display in full sun in northern gardens or part shade farther south. 'Gouchaultii' is similar to but more vigorous and less bright yellow than 'Spaethii'. The dark winter stems can be generously described as subtle. A shy grower, this dogwood is fairly susceptible to leaf spot.

***Cornus alba* 'Hessei',** an older form from the Hesse nursery in Germany, is uncommon in cultivation. Mike Buffin, formerly of the Sir Harold Hillier Gardens and Arboretum, indicated that he has seen only two plants of 'Hessei': one at Hillier's and one at the Royal Botanic Garden, Edinburgh (the source of the Hillier plant). The Edinburgh plant has since died; it was received directly from the Hesse nursery where it originated as a seedling in a batch of *Crataegus* seed from the St. Petersburg Botanic Garden. 'Hessei' is a compact and very slow growing form of *Cornus alba*. Stem color on new, more vigorous shoots is similar to the species, while older shoots resemble somewhat the shoots of *C. alba* 'Kesselringii': they are slightly gnarled with very short internode spacing and are purple-black to deep purple. Leaves are lanceolate, typically wedge-shaped with a slender tip, and are about 1.5 inches (4 cm) long, sometimes longer; they emerge green and are slightly crinkled. As summer progresses the foliage turns a deep purple before dropping. The Hillier plant flowers and produces seed each year. Flowers are white, occasionally tinged pink, typical of *C. alba*, with slightly flattened cymes which are quite in keeping with the overall compact habit of the plant. Fruits begin white before ripening to bluish black and are produced in low numbers. This selection is very difficult to root and so is propagated by grafting. The Hillier plant was grafted onto *C. alba* 'Sibirica'.

Cornus alba 'Kesselringii'

***Cornus alba* 'Kesselringii'** is not the showiest of the bunch: the winter stems are dark purple-brown and seem to blend into the woodwork. Summer stems are a bit more purple-green. The leaves emerge with a distinctly dark red-green cast but alas, the effect is short lived. In Paul's experience, this selection seems to be the most canker susceptible form commonly grown. Flowers are sometimes described as being suffused with pink. In actuality, the petals are creamy white with the coloration coming from the dark purple-pink pedicels. The plant is not overly vigorous, eventually growing 7–8 feet (2.1–2.4 m) tall and 5 feet (1.5 m) wide. 'Kesselringii' originated from a seed lot from *C. alba* 'Sibirica' at the St. Petersburg Botanic Garden in 1905.

Cornus alba **Regnzam'** (Red Gnome™), a compact and fine-textured selection, is described as growing to 3 feet (90 cm) tall and 4–5 feet (1.2–1.5 m) wide with bright red winter stems and burgundy fall foliage color. While it will likely grow to a larger size than the original description, it does have a finer texture than most other *C. alba* selections. Leaf spot susceptibility is unknown. This dogwood was introduced by Lake County Nursery in Ohio.

Cornus alba **'Rosenthall',** a late nineteenth-century selection from the Rosenthal Nursery of Albern, Austria, offers large, bold leaves with gray-green centers and a bright yellow gold margin.

Cornus alba **'Ruby',** introduced by the U.S. Soil Conservation Service, has good red fall color and heavy fruit crop. Because it is a seed-produced cultivar, this selection shows some variation from plant to plant.

Cornus alba **'Siberian Pearls'** was selected for heavy flowering and large masses of white fruits, eventually maturing to deep blue. In the real world of the garden, this selection does not seem to be much more floriferous than most others. It has a decidedly fine branch texture and grows to 6 feet (1.8 m) tall and wide.

Cornus alba **'Sibirica'** is among the brightest colored winter stems of the bunch. A second distinguishing feature often listed is bluish fruit color. It would be interesting to see how blue fruit separates this selection from almost any other as most display this trait. To make a long story longer, this selection is best labeled as "buyer, beware!" There seems to be complete confusion as to the true identity of this selection. Several nurseries have been reported to pick the best-colored seedlings from the field and sell them as 'Sibirica'. In 1967 Donald Wyman reported that the Arnold Arboretum had obtained plants so named from nearly three-dozen commercial sources and found most to be misidentified. Most were *C. baileyi*, *C. stolonifera*, or *C. amomum*. The arboretum apparently identified the correct taxon and redistributed plants to growers. Alas, a futile effort because 35 years later we find ourselves in the same boat. Interestingly, in the article, Wyman listed the plant as a variety (*C. alba* var. *sibirica*) rather than as a cultivar ('Sibirica'). Depending on written report or labeled plant, one could consider *C. alba* 'Sibirica', 'Sibirica Bloodgood', and 'Westonbirt' one and the same. They are all so confused, all purported to be the most brilliant of the bunch, and unfortunately, none of the type specimens still exist. Occasionally, 'Regnzam' (Red Gnome™) is listed under the name 'Sibirica Red Gnome'. Original descriptions of 'Sibirica' list it as having broad leaves, coral pink stems, and limited vigor.

Cornus alba **'Sibirica Variegata'** is another cultivar with tremendous confusion. Lake County Nursery of northern Ohio lists it as one of their new selections. Krüssman (1984) listed it as an 1867 introduction similar to 'Argenteo-marginata' but with larger leaves and more gray-green centers.

Cornus alba **'Snow Pearls'** was selected for heavy crops of white fruit.

Cornus alba **'Spaethii'** has brilliantly toned yellow margins with green or green-red centers. It is a bit limited in the vigor category but well worth the wait. 'Spaethii' holds the foliage color best in northern gardens. It does develop some stem canker as do most cultivars of the species, and especially the variegated selections. Leaf spot seems to be minimal. Dirr (1990) provides an interesting tale to propose the origin of the cultivar introduced in 1889 in Spaeth, Berlin:

> The cultivar originated on the stem of the species, on which was grafted a white-variegated scion; the scion died and just beneath the point of union a yellow-variegated shoot developed; it could be that some callus formation had taken place before the scion died and the resultant yellow-foliaged form was, in fact, a graft-chimera.

Cornus alba **'Staltouch'** (Touch of Elegance™), a sport of *C. alba* 'Argenteo-marginata', has white variegated leaves and compact growth. It is slightly smaller growing than *C. alba* 'Bailhalo' (Ivory Halo™). 'Staltouch' apparently reverts to the green form fairly regularly and has not proven to be much of a grower in general. It is rarely seen. Selected by Don Stallard of Madison, Ohio. Plant patent number PP10,771.

Cornus alba **'Stdazam'** (Strawberry Daiquiri®) is a white-edged variegated selection that shows medium green centers and irregular creamy white margins. Winter stems are a deep red-maroon. Plants grow to 5 feet (1.5 m) tall and wide or slightly greater. This dogwood was introduced by Lake County Nursery of Ohio and described by the company as a replacement for *C. alba* 'Argenteo-marginata'. The two are so similar, it is hard to understand how one is better than the other.

Cornus alba **'Variegata'** is a name of little horticultural standing.

Cornus amomum
SILKY DOGWOOD

Cornus amomum forms a suckering shrub 8–12 feet (2.4–3.6 m) tall. It tends to become sparse at the base with age. In general, this rather scraggly grower is best relegated to the naturalized planting or reforestation projects in its native range. In the wild, it provides cover for wildlife and fruit for birds, but it generally lacks any of the more ornamental characteristics of its showier cousins.

Young stems are purplish with some hint of green, and second-year stems become mostly brown to gray-brown. Older stems are flat gray and of little ornamental appeal. Pith is brown. The leaves are 2–4 inches (5–10 cm) long and 1–2 inches (2.5–5 cm) wide, ovate to elliptic, acute or acuminate at the tip with an acute or rounded base. They are dark green with an occasional purple tint to the veins above; glaucous beneath with occasional tufts of brown hairs on the veins. Petioles are 0.5 inch (12 mm) long. Overall, the effect is a rather fine texture. Inflorescences are quite small compared to its close relations. Small, creamy to yellow-white perfect flowers are produced in flat-topped cymes 1.5–2 inches (4–5

Cornus amomum

Cornus amomum

cm) in diameter, slightly before *Cornus alba* and *C. stolonifera*. The fruit can be a bright gray-blue on some, but is most often blue-black. The drupes are 0.25 inch (6 mm) in diameter, borne in small clusters in late summer, and are quickly eaten by birds.

Cornus amomum is best in moist, partially shaded sites but will take full sun if the gardener is absolutely bent on having one. There are so many wonderful shrubs on the planet, it would be difficult to believe that one could not find a better plant for just about any location. Native throughout the eastern seaboard from New York to Georgia and west to Kentucky and Tennessee.

Seed propagation of *Cornus amomum* requires a longer cold treatment than most; 90–180 days will work, with the longer treatments resulting in more uniform germination. Summer softwood cuttings root well in three to five weeks with 1000 ppm IBA treatment. Hardwood cuttings do not root as easily as those of *C. alba* but will root 75 percent with 3000 ppm IBA.

Cornus amomum 'Indigo', selected from wild-collected seed in the central United States, is a seed-produced cultivar from the U.S. Soil Conservation Service.

Cornus asperifolia
ROUGH LEAF DOGWOOD

Cornus asperifolia is essentially *C. amomum* with more pubescence on stems, leaves, buds, and so forth. The leaf is more uniformly ovate and lacks the acuminate apex. Stems retain some of the purplish red a season or two longer than on *C. amomum*. White pith in the stems and fruit tends to be whiter than the typical blue of *C. amomum*. The range of *C. asperifolia* tends to overlap that of *C. amomum* but extends farther north, south, and west. The species is typically found in the eastern and central United States.

Cornus asperifolia var. drummondii is distinguished from the species by greater pubescence on the upper portion of the leaf blade and by a slightly more tapered leaf shape. This is a definite up-and-comer in the plant world. It can be pruned up to a great little tree if desired and, given its adaptability, could be quite useful as a small street tree. Bill Hendricks of Klyn Nursery, Perry, Ohio, has been growing a form with creamy yellow flowers and fruit. The selection, as yet unnamed, makes an outstanding little tree.

Cornus australis

Cornus australis, a shrubby species from Asia Minor, forms a plant 8–10 feet (2.4–3.6 m) tall and wide and generally reminiscent of *C. sanguinea*. The stems are greenish purple on new wood, fading to gray on stems older than about three years. This dogwood is not one of the showiest of the group with inflorescences no more than about 2 inches (5 cm) across. The species can be separated from many of the other similar shrubby species by the purple fruit. Zone 6.

Cornus australis var. koenigii has somewhat larger leaves and longer petioles.

Cornus bretschneideri

Cornus bretschneideri is a large version of *C. alba*, to 15 feet (4.5 m) tall. The winter stems lack the same full red punch of Tatarian dogwood, tending more toward yellow in winter with some red toward the tips. The ovate leaves are 2–4 inches (5–10 cm) long and show significant undulation along the margin and a distinctly acuminate tip. Fruit is blue-black. Native to China. Zone 5.

Cornus glabrata
BROWN DOGWOOD, WESTERN CORNEL

If ever a plant was in serious need of an image consultant, this would be it. Not many buyers beat down the doors of the garden center for a plant with a name like brown dogwood. Western cornel might be a better bet here. *Cornus glabrata* at 12 to 15 feet (3.6–4.5 m) tall is a lax grower with long looping and somewhat arching branches, a description that may leave one thinking, graceful. Alas, sprawling and scraggly might be more accurate. The stems, generally red-brown, and the inflorescences, 1–1.5 inches (2.5–4 cm) in diameter, don't do much to stir the soul either. Fruit is white to bluish white. This species is best used as a naturalizing shrub for a place that can afford the real estate. It is native to the western United States. Zone 5b or 6.

Cornus obliqua

Cornus oblonga

Cornus obliqua

Cornus obliqua, a member of the *C. amomum* clan, differs primarily in the lax branching, occasional yellow tint to the new stems, and the more narrowly ovate leaves. Most other characteristics are quite similar. The natural distribution of this species tends more northerly and westerly compared with *C. amomum*. It is often found in damp fields and the edge of woodlands from Quebec to Kansas and south to southern Illinois. This dogwood is sometimes listed as *C. amomum* subsp. *obliqua*.

Cornus oblonga

Cornus oblonga—you had to expect at least one "also ran" for the list. This species is listed here because it really doesn't fit elsewhere. It is probably most closely related to some of the Asian members of the *C. alba* clan; however, being an evergreen in USDA hardiness zones 8b–9, it seems to want to be separated, at least for this garden treatment of the genus.

This species produces plants 15–20 feet (4.5–6 m) tall as either large shrubs or small trees. It is easily separated from most other dogwoods by virtue of the four-angled stems covered with a yellow-tan felt. Leaves are ovate, acuminate, and deep glossy green and apparently not tolerant of much more than an occasional hard freeze. The flowers are produced in late summer, in terminal panicles up to 3 inches (7.5 cm) long and wide, consisting of small yellowish white, four-petaled individual flowers. Fruit is a small longish black drupe.

Cornus paucinervis

Cornus paucinervis, from central China, is rarely found in commerce but occasionally encountered in botanic gardens. Unfortunately, most of the plants encountered tend to be *C. stolonifera*, *C. alba*, or other closely related species. Generally, *C. paucinervis* forms a slightly arching plant, 6–10 feet (1.8–3 m) tall, with weakly colored red-brown stems. Young stems are distinctly four-angled, separating this species from many others. The early to midsummer flowers are similar to many of those of many close relatives. Fruit matures to black and is sparsely set. Leaves are 2–3 inches (5–7.5 cm) long, ovate to obovate, with adpressed hairs above and below. Most plants hold their leaves quite late into the fall and show little fall foliage color. Some southern seed strains show almost evergreen nature. Ernest H. Wilson (1913) described this species as being found commonly in central China, typically along the water's edge in low-lying areas. Zones 5–8.

Cornus pumila

Cornus pumila, a densely branched shrub, grows to about 5 feet (1.5 m) tall and a bit more in width, although it takes its sweet time getting there. Its major claim to

Cornus pumila

Cornus pumila

fame is that nobody knows much about it. Really, this species is often listed as "origin unknown" and is so listed in Alfred Rehder's indispensable *Manual of Cultivated Trees and Shrubs* (1990). It has been cultivated since the late nineteenth century.

Think of *Cornus pumila* as *C. alba*, reduced in stature, with smaller inflorescences and little to no red in the winter stems. The new emerging leaves have a red tinge, which might be considered interesting. The species also seems to be fairly free from stem canker problems. Leaf spot can be a considerable problem in more humid climates.

The most amazing aspect of this species is that it has somehow become ingrained in American horticulture. Not that one will find this everywhere in gardens and garden centers, but it is far more available than some of its relatives that may be considered far showier. The bottom line seems to be that it is a nice serviceable little plant in the northern tier. In the southern United States, it is not quite as dependable. Zones 4–7.

Cornus racemosa
GRAY DOGWOOD

Cornus racemosa forms a large finely twiggy mass of upright gray stems. Like many of the shrub dogwoods, this one brings to mind the word "utilitarian." And in few cases is it more appropriate than here. Gray dogwood typically grows 8–10 (2.4–3 m) feet tall but can spread almost indefinitely from profuse suckers. One would curse the day they planted it as a companion plant in a perennial bed! Gray dogwood can also be pruned up to a small tree. If so grown, it would make a nice little tree for impossible urban landscapes. A specimen in the collection at Bernheim Arboretum, Clermont, Kentucky, with a 6-inch (15-cm) caliper single stem, while not lighting anyone's socks afire, is definitely thriving and casting shade in miserable conditions. Lake County Nursery of Ohio also has a couple of selections that they typically grow into nice little tree-form specimens.

Cornus foemina, which has now been rolled into *C. racemosa* by most taxonomists, used to be separated as the larger growing form of the latter. This may be the lineage of some of the more treelike forms.

Narrow elliptic leaves of dark flat green generally remain in good condition through most of the summer. There is little or no leaf spot to worry about here. Fall foliage is nothing to write home about. Fruit typically mature to white and do not last long into the fall; however, the peduncles, or supporting structures for the fruit, are pinkish red and may persist into early winter. Many landscape architecture students have used the structures as tiny shade trees for landscape models.

Culturally, gray dogwood requires as close to nothing as one will find in the plant kingdom. Given that its native range spreads from eastern Canada, down the eastern seaboard to Georgia and west to Nebraska, it should be of little surprise that the species is so adaptable. It transplants readily and will tolerate full sun to full shade. While it prefers moist soils, it will grow from dry clay to soggy fields and rarely seems to complain. The most significant malady is sawfly larvae; this pest may attack the leaves in early summer, stripping the entire plant in a couple days. In general, gray dogwood is best left to naturalizing, bank stabilization, and other utilitarian uses.

Cornus racemosa

The naturally occurring hybrid of *Cornus racemosa* and *C. obliqua*, *C.* ×*arnoldiana* looks essentially like *C. racemosa* with heavy short pubescence on the lower surface of the leaves and purple in the older bark. It is generally found in the upper Midwest.

Seed propagation of *Cornus racemosa* can be a bit trying. Seeds treated with concentrated sulfuric acid for two to four hours and then cold stratified for four months can be expected to germinate at about 60 to 75 percent. Softwood cuttings are a bit more difficult than many related species. Dirr (1998) reports best results with 1000 ppm NAA in talc yielding 100 percent rooting in 37 days, while 80 ppm IBA yielded only 60 percent. Hardwood cuttings treated with 3000 ppm IBA can be expected to root about 60 percent. Zones 3–8.

Cornus racemosa **'Cinderella'**, a rarely seen selection, has leaves showing dark green centers surrounded by blotches of gray-green and margins of yellow, fading to cream. In 1983, nurseryman Lanny Rawdon of Arborvillage Farm, Holt, Missouri, discovered a variegated sport on a naturally occurring plant of *C. racemosa* growing on his farm. The original sport was named 'Heaven Sent' and propagated, but showed considerable instability in the variegation. Subsequently, one branch of the selection was identified as being more stable and was propagated and named 'Cinderella'. This dogwood grows to about 15 feet (4.5 m) tall and wide. Plant patent number PP7,766 was awarded in January 1992. A variegated selection of such a bomb-proof species would seem to be an instant hit. Yet, 'Cinderella' is rarely, if ever, seen in the trade. Makes one wonder about the stability.

Cornus racemosa **'Cuyzam'** (Cuyahoga™) is one of a series of cultivars introduced by Lake County Nursery in Ohio under the name of Counties of Ohio™. This selection with deep glossy green leaves and bright white fruit was selected particularly for use as a small street tree. It grows 12–15 feet (3.6–4.5 m) tall and 10–12 feet (3–3.6 m) wide. When growing for small tree use, propagate from cuttings to reduce sucker growth.

Cornus racemosa **'Geazam'** (Geauga®), another of the Counties of Ohio™ selections, shows reddish new foliage on an upright plant 8 feet (2.4 m) tall and 4 feet (1.2 m) wide. It has glossy dark green foliage through the summer.

Cornus racemosa **'Hurzam'** (Huron®), a Counties of Ohio™ selection, is described as showing excellent compact growth to 3 or 4 feet (90–120 cm) tall and wide. It has reddish new growth and good spot resistance. 'Hurzam' is the most compact of the *C. racemosa* selections.

Cornus racemosa (above and above right)

Cornus racemosa 'Cinderella'

Cornus racemosa 'Cuyzam'

***Cornus racemosa* 'Jade'** (Snow Mantle™), a stout, somewhat tree form, is sometimes listed under *C. foemina*.

***Cornus racemosa* 'Mahzam'** (Mahoning™), a Lake County Nursery introduction, seems to be a rather vigorously suckering and spreading form. It is not distinct from typical *C. racemosa*.

***Cornus racemosa* 'Muszam'** (Muskingum®) is described as a low, lax-growing form up to 2 feet (60 cm) tall and 4 feet (1.2 m) wide with rather narrow, light green leaves. The shortest of the Counties of Ohio™ selections, it is not as dense and compact as Huron®.

***Cornus racemosa* 'Ottzam'** (Ottawa™), a somewhat upright form to 10 to 12 feet (3–3.6 m) tall and half as wide, has very dark glossy foliage. It is a good selection for production as a small tree.

***Cornus racemosa* 'Slavin's Dwarf'** is often mistakenly listed as *C. ×slavinii*, a naturally occurring hybrid of *C. rugosa* and *C. stolonifera*. The cultivar in question here is a small, compact form that supposedly grows to only 2 or 3 feet (60–90 cm) tall.

Cornus rugosa
ROUND LEAVED DOGWOOD, ROUGH LEAVED DOGWOOD

Cornus rugosa is a coarse, shrubby species growing 8–10 feet (2.4–3 m) tall with an equal width. It lacks the colorful stems of many of its showier brethren but does make a reasonable naturalizing shrub. Young stems are green, changing to purple, with a distinctly rough or warty surface. This dogwood has the flat cymose inflorescences of most of its relatives. Probably the best feature of the species is the sometimes pale, almost steely blue fruit, which don't last long but can be nice in the late summer. Fall color is occasionally a reasonable red in sunny sites. Zone 4.

Cornus sanguinea
BLOODTWIG OR COMMON DOGWOOD

Cornus sanguinea forms a large and somewhat coarse heavily suckering shrub to 8 to 12 feet (2.4–3.6 m) tall. This European native is generally found on neutral to chalky soils, and overall is quite adaptable.

While there are some notable exceptions, most plants show dull gray older canes with purple younger stems. The purple is most pronounced on the sunny side of the plant. Some of the better selections show brilliant orange, yellow, red, and coral-colored stems, typically with more red on the sunny side.

Leaves are typically deep green, 2–3.5 inches (5–9 cm) long, ovate, with a rounded base. Petioles are 0.25–0.5 inch (6–12 mm) long. Fall color is typically wanting. Oddly, some of the bright barked forms tend to show significant yellowing of the summer foliage in warmer zones. This seems unrelated to any pathology. This dogwood appears to be a very heavy feeder, and ample nitrogen often helps. Leaf spot can be significant in some climates and, as with *Cornus alba*, the warmer and drier the climate, the worse the problem.

Flowers are creamy white, lacking in fragrance, and borne in flat masses up to 2 inches (5 cm) across. They attract a wide range of bees and other assorted pollinators. Generally, they are not particularly overwhelming in full bloom. Fruit are black drupes that ripen in late summer and are soon taken by birds.

The only significant historical use for *Cornus sanguinea* is young stems having been used as butcher's skewers.

Seed propagation requires three months of warm and three months of cold stratification. Softwood cuttings root readily with 1000 to 3000 ppm IBA. One study reported 75 percent rooting of hardwood cuttings with no pretreatment.

Cornus sanguinea 'Compressa'

***Cornus sanguinea* 'Compressa'** is a bizarre little upright plant that some have described as dwarf despite the fact that it can grow to 6 to 8 feet (1.8–2.4 m) tall after considerable time. It has very short internodes and densely crowded branches, almost all strongly ascending. Leaves are slightly larger than a quarter and of an almost cardboard constitution. Typical leaf color is gray-green to dark green and veins are deeply impressed. This plant is definitely not going to win any beauty contest. The stems are gray-brown and there is little to no fall foliage color. Once established, plants may develop considerable suckering from the roots. Plants rarely, if ever, flower and fruit. Without a doubt, this is a plant geek's plant. Piecing together various conversations with observations of plants offered for sale in European nurseries (the plant is rarely listed in the United States), it seems that most dogwoods seen under the name *C. alba* 'Hessei' are actually *C. sanguinea* 'Compressa'. According to Krüssman (1984), this plant was selected by Magyar at the School of Horticulture in Budapest, Hungary, in the 1960s.

***Cornus sanguinea* 'Greenlight'** is listed in several sources without description.

***Cornus sanguinea* 'Midwinter Fire'** is without a doubt one of the best cultivars of *C. sanguinea*. It and 'Winter Beauty' are distinct selections that have been entirely confused in the trade in the United States and overseas as well. The history of their discovery and introduction to commerce is based on the 1995 *Dendroflora* article by de Jong and Ilsink. The original plant in question was discovered by H. Venhorst of Mechelen, Netherlands, in a German garden in about 1980. All propagation material was bought by Van den Dool Cultures BV, Boskoop, Netherlands, and named 'Midwinter Fire' in 1990.

'Midwinter Fire' forms a broad upright shrub with young stems colored brilliant orange-yellow during winter and clear red at the sunny sides. The stems return to yellow-green in summer and, as with other brightly colored dogwood species, the bark color changes rapidly, coinciding with leaf emergence in spring and leaf drop in fall. Summer leaves are a bright green and can sometimes go a bit yellow in early summer. Fall foliage color can be a splendid yellow.

Although 'Midwinter Fire' and 'Winter Beauty' are similar in stem color and foliage, they differ in a way that should be of particular interest to gardeners. 'Midwinter Fire' is a robust grower, rapidly taking root, spreading by suckering growth and filling significant acreage. Its winter stem color tends much more to the yellow-orange. 'Winter Beauty' is a shy grower and does not show the heavy suckering growth. It will make excellent growth in time, but takes a while to get in the mood. Stem color on 'Winter Beauty' tends more toward the reds and corals.

According to de Jong and Ilsink, 'Midwinter Fire' may be the same as *Cornus sanguinea* 'Beteramsii', brought into the trade by Beterams Nursery in Geldern, Germany.

***Cornus sanguinea* 'Mietzschii'** is a variegated form with varying amounts of green, gray, and white. It has excellent fall foliage color varying pink and red. It was introduced before 1900. Rarely offered for sale.

***Cornus sanguinea* 'Variegata'**, as the name implies, is a variegated form. It differs from 'Mietzschii' in having white and yellow splashes rather than white and gray.

***Cornus sanguinea* 'Viridissima'** may very well be for the gardener who has everything . . . every plant that is. But if someone was interested in a green-stemmed form with green fruit, here it is.

***Cornus sanguinea* 'Winter Beauty'** (synonyms 'Anny', 'Anny's', 'Magic Flame', 'Winter Flame') was raised and named by Andre van Nijnatten of Zundert, Netherlands, in 1987. It grows to be an upright shrub with bright red stems and occa-

Cornus sanguinea 'Winter Beauty'

sional shades of yellow and orange. Fall foliage is an excellent clear yellow. As noted earlier, this selection can be distinguished from 'Midwinter Fire' by winter stem color and vigor of young plants. 'Winter Beauty' is not as robust a grower and does not sucker as profusely as its close cousin. 'Winter Beauty' also shows more red in the winter bark. This plant was first described in *Dendroflora* 24 (1987) as the winner of the best novelty plant award at the Flora Nova in 1987 by the Royal Boskoop Horticultural Society.

Cornus sessilis
BLACK FRUITED DOGWOOD

Cornus sessilis is an uncommon native of north central California. It fits the description of many of the members treated in this section, although it shares a similar chromosome number with *C. mas*. This shrubby dogwood reaches 12–15 feet (3.6–4.5 m) tall and has green new stems that eventually turn a grayish brown. The creamy white flowers are borne in small umbels up to almost 2 inches (5 cm) in diameter and have the odd characteristic of being surrounded by sets of three protective bracts through the winter. The leaves can develop a nice red to burgundy in the fall. The black-fruited dogwood is aptly named as the small drupes begin somewhat dull red and eventually ripen to a bright shiny black. They are taken quickly by birds. This species is typically found in redwood forests as an understory plant. It is rarely seen or planted. Zones 7–10.

Cornus stolonifera
RED OSIER, RED-STEMMED DOGWOOD, SNAKEROOT

Think of *Cornus stolonifera* as a shorter, wider growing cousin of *C. alba*. *Cornus stolonifera* is more of a broad-spreading, heavily suckering shrub that will grow to 6 feet (1.8 m) tall and 10 feet (3 m) or so wide. The suckering habit makes it a bit tough to use this dogwood in smaller scale landscapes. Winter stems are deep to bright red, occasionally yellow, and as with all its relatives, the stem color is best on young, vigorous plants.

Bright to medium green leaves are thin in texture. Fall color can be a reasonable red above with whitish gray beneath. Generally, the leaves are a bit tattered by late summer or early fall and thus don't make much of a show. The petiole is 0.5–1 inch (12–25 mm) long.

Flowers are ivory to creamy white, borne in corymbs 2–3 inches (5–7.5 cm) wide. They are somewhat fragrant but not necessarily pleasantly so. Fruit is a

Cornus stolonifera (above, above right, and below)

white drupe, 0.25 inch (6 mm) in diameter, that can make somewhat of a show in fall against the occasionally good red fall foliage. The stone is large, almost rounded with a blunt or rounded base. This contrasts with the oblong fruit of *Cornus alba* that is distinctly tapered at both ends.

In the wild, *Cornus stolonifera* is found along streams, in old fields and occasionally in forest openings. The species along with its varieties ranges essentially from coast to coast in North America. Very cold hardy, *C. stolonifera* can go from USDA hardiness zone 2 south to about zone 7, but in the southern part of the range it is most often found at higher elevations. Still, in zones 7 and 8 it is a better choice than *C. alba*.

In warm regions, plants can suffer significantly from stem canker problems. Excellent drainage can lessen the severity of the problem. Essentially, the farther south one progresses, the more critical it becomes to provide good drainage. Leaf spot can also be a significant problem in the landscape. Generally, leaf spot is worse in areas with hot dry summers.

Cornus stolonifera makes a wonderful mass planting, especially when backed by dark evergreens. It brings cheer and color to the somber hues of the winter landscape. The yellow-stemmed selections do a wonderful job of adding a bit of the unexpected to the landscape.

The only culinary use of the species noted in historical texts, and it is a bit of a stretch here to call its use culinary, is the inner bark having been mixed with tobacco and smoked by native tribes of the Great Lakes region and central United States.

Propagation is as listed for *Cornus alba*.

Cornus stolonifera f. baileyi (synonyms 'Baileyi', 'Bailey') has been listed as a cultivar, form, variety, and even occasionally a species. Paul honestly cannot tell it from straight *C. stolonifera* and he dissected more than a few hundred of these as part of his dissertation work! In literature, it is described as having more brown-red color in winter stems and a growth habit like that of a spreading *C. alba*. Plants Paul has seen listed as this selection tend to have more brown in the stems, but the variation is so great, this criterion is on fairly shaky ground. For some reason, this form has been in catalogs in midwestern U.S. nurseries for some time. We have no idea why it gained such recognition there. With the increased popularity of the newer bright-stemmed cultivars, f. *baileyi* is beginning to disappear from the marketplace—probably not such a bad thing in the long run.

Cornus stolonifera 'Bergesson's Compact', as the name implies, is slightly more compact and seems not to develop the sprawling habit of older plants of the species. Ultimate size is approximately 5 feet (1.5 m) tall and wide. Leaves are a bit smaller than those of the species, and the inflorescences are about half the typical size.

***Cornus stolonifera* 'Bud's Yellow'** has yellow to yellow-green stems and was introduced by Boughen Nurseries, Saskatchewan, Canada. It was originally reported to be highly resistant to stem canker, but Paul has seen significant canker problems in numerous specimens. To him, it is as susceptible to canker as is *C. stolonifera* 'Flaviramea'. Although often listed as a selection of *C. alba*, it should be listed as *C. stolonifera*. The plant grows to about 6 feet (1.8 m) tall and 8 feet (2.4 m) wide and does not sucker heavily.

***Cornus stolonifera* 'Cardinal'** has brilliant red winter stems but is otherwise typical for the species. Selected by Harold Pellet of the Minnesota Landscape Arboretum, Chanhassen, this dogwood originated from a provenance collection of the species. Of all the seedlings grown in the screening, this one exhibited the best red winter stem color. In the southern part of its range (zones 7–8), winter stem color is more of a yellow-orange than the brilliant reds seen in northern landscapes.

***Cornus stolonifera* 'Cheyenne'**, generally listed as a selection of var. *coloradensis*, has rich, deep red stems, not as bright as 'Cardinal' but still quite nice. It tops out at about 5 feet (1.5 m) tall in most instances.

Cornus stolonifera 'Bergesson's Compact'

Cornus stolonifera 'Cardinal'

Cornus stolonifera **var. *coloradensis*** is a western and central North American variant with brown stems, smaller and narrower leaves, and blue-white fruit. Not much of a calling card for a plant grown primarily for its bright stem color.

Cornus stolonifera **'Elongata'** is described as a green-stemmed form with longer-than-normal leaves, distinctly tapered at both ends.

Cornus stolonifera **'Flaviramea'** (synonym 'Lutea') is the classic yellow stem form. Dirr (1998) listed this as first offered by the Spaeth Nursery, Germany, 1890–1900, which received it from the Arnold Arboretum. It shows typical growth for the species, with bright yellow stems in winter, fading to green in summer. This cultivar is supposedly more susceptible to stem canker problems than other cultivars, but saying this is sort of like claiming one's teenager is more attentive than most: sure it is a matter of degrees, but the spread isn't that great. This is a fabulous plant if used appropriately. The impact of the bright cheerful stems against evergreen foliage or otherwise drab bare mulch is more than adequate tradeoff for the lack of spring and summer zip. Aside from the stems, it is a particularly glossy leafed form. When the foliage remains in good condition through to the bitter end

Cornus stolonifera 'Flaviramea'

of summer, it provides an excellent dark glossy foil for the white fruit. When Paul taught the nursery management class at the University of Maine, he and his students used to graft this form onto sticks of the species and stick the cuttings. Thus they would be rooting and grafting on the same sticks to create an odd little horticultural conversation piece.

***Cornus stolonifera* 'Garden Glow',** another selection from Harold Pellet, is a low spreading form that will eventually grow 4–5 feet (1.2–1.5 m) tall and 6–7 feet (1.8–2.1 m) wide. Its primary attribute is the crop of soft chartreuse (if that is possible) broad flat leaves. In full sun, the color is more brilliant yellow-gold but in southern areas the color quickly begins to burn. In a shady spot in Paul's Louisville (Kentucky) garden, the leaves

Cornus stolonifera 'Flaviramea'

Cornus stolonifera 'Garden Glow'

held up beautifully and added a subtle bright spot against *Mahonia bealei* and *Hosta* 'Bressingham Blue'. Stems are green in summer and bright pinkish red in winter.

This selection originated as a chance seedling from a seed lot received from a botanic garden in eastern Europe. The seeds were labeled as coming from *Cornus hessei*. Unfortunately, that species does not seem to exist. The closest in nomenclatural terms would be *C. alba* 'Hessei', an old selection from the well-known German nursery of the same name. The story continues. *Cornus alba* 'Hessei' is an extremely dwarf and slow-growing form that to Paul's knowledge does not flower. So we have a bit of a conundrum. Having grown the plant for several years, it seems very much like *C. stolonifera* to Paul. A plant patent has been applied for.

***Cornus stolonifera* 'Hedgerow's Gold'** is a variegated form with dark green, light green, and gold mixed to produce a very pretty leaf, at least for the first few weeks of the season. However, once the leaf spot begins, it is a nasty sight indeed. It almost looks as though a cranky gardener extinguished too many cigarettes on the leaves. Plants Paul has observed in gardens indicate that good garden sanitation may help here. Most often, the foliage stays nice and clean for the first few seasons; however, over time, the inoculum must build up to a critical concentration to cause the eventual problem. The spot is not as much of a problem in areas with cooler summers. This is a very vigorous form for a variegated cultivar.

Cornus stolonifera 'Hedgerow's Gold'

***Cornus stolonifera* 'Isanti'** is a slightly smaller and finer textured form introduced by the Minnesota Landscape Arboretum. The flowers, leaves, and internodes are about two-thirds the size of typical *C. stolonifera*. 'Isanti' develops considerable leaf spot in warmer areas, but in northern landscapes is quite nice. Plants mature to about 5 feet (1.5 m) tall and wide.

***Cornus stolonifera* 'Kelseyi',** from its descriptions, seems like the greatest thing since duct tape (or is that duck tape?). This dwarf plant matures at less than 2 feet (60 cm) tall and 3 feet (90 cm) wide. It is fine textured and does not spread extensively. All sounds good so far. Unfortunately, those are all the kind things that one can say about the cultivar. It is

Cornus stolonifera 'Isanti'

Cornus stolonifera 'Kelseyi'

without doubt the most leaf spot susceptible of all dogwoods. The stem color is best described as lacking, and the plant flowers sparsely if at all. Fall foliage color could be described as mulch. There may be somewhere on the planet that this is not the case. This selection was introduced by the Kelsey Highlands Nursery of East Boxford, Massachusetts, in 1927. Several early descriptions wax eloquent about this selection. The only assessment Paul can make is that possibly the leaf spot inoculum was not as widespread in the early 1900s.

***Cornus stolonifera* 'Nitida',** an essentially green-stemmed, somewhat upright growing selection with glossy summer foliage, is not often seen in commerce.

Cornus stolonifera* var. *occidentalis is the western form listed by some authorities as *C. occidentalis*. It shows most of the characteristics of the species but is generally a larger plant, sometimes reaching small tree stature. The winter stems tend more toward a dark purple or burgundy rather than the bright red of the species.

Cornus stolonifera 'Silver and Gold'

To give the reader a sense of the confusion with this member (and a few others) of the group, one botanical reference describes the leaf tips as blunt or sharp pointed, and the leaf lower surfaces as being pubescent or glabrous. Are you getting a clear picture? The fruit is white. Zones 5–6. To make matters worse, a hybrid of *C. stolonifera* and the western variety, *C. ×californica*, creek dogwood, is described as having leaves that are both pointed and downy! It is most often listed as occurring in the Pacific Northwest.

***Cornus stolonifera* 'Rosco',** a small growing, fine-textured form with weakly gold spring leaves, is identical to plants sold under 'Kelsey's Gold' according to some sources.

***Cornus stolonifera* 'Silver and Gold'** is a real winner in the landscape if one can overlook the canker problems inherent in the species, problems that are minimized with adequate drainage. Paul could find a spot for this selection in just about any garden. 'Flaviramea'-like yellow winter stems are followed by white-edged green leaves throughout the summer.

Cornus stolonifera 'Silver and Gold'

'Silver and Gold' is excellent in masses or as a specimen, and it works very well with the deep hues of Siberian iris. It tends to be a bit shorter than other forms of *C. stolonifera*. Leaf spot varies considerably from site to site but can be severe in some places. This cultivar does best in a little shade for highest quality foliage. It originated as a branch sport on 'Flaviramea' and was introduced in 1987 by the Mt. Cuba Center for the Study of Piedmont Flora in Greenville, Delaware.

***Cornus stolonifera* 'Sunshine',** if one subscribes to such splitting, is most properly attributed to var. *occidentalis*, the western variety of the species. It is a large form, 8–10 feet (2.4–3 m) tall, with variously yellow, gold, and chartreuse leaves that may be all one color (most common) or occasionally of varying hues. Paul was high on this cultivar during the first few years he grew it in Kentucky, but after several years, the leaf spot began to creep in and what was spring riches turned rapidly to summer rags. The foliage burn and leaf spot marched in and made what was a nice display, a horrid sight that was difficult to forget. Ultimately, this cultivar gives 'Kelseyi' a healthy run for its leadership roll in the leaf-spot-susceptible

Cornus stolonifera 'Sunshine'

hall of fame, but Paul saw a late summer planting in Seattle in 2001 and it was not only clean as a whistle, it was looking fabulous in combination with late summer purple asters. Apparently this is another one of those east-west things. 'Sunshine' was introduced by the University of Washington Arboretum.

***Cornus stolonifera* 'Variegata',** of which Paul has only seen one plant so labeled, is a weakly edge-variegated (white) form, upright and fairly vigorous. We could not track down its origin.

***Cornus stolonifera* 'White Gold'** has yellow-green stems and variegated leaves. Foliage tends to have more of a graded cream to gold to green arrangement compared to 'Silver and Gold'. It is sometimes sold under the name 'White Spot'. This cultivar is more commonly seen in Europe than in the United States.

Cornus walteri
WALTER DOGWOOD

Cornus walteri is relatively uncommon, though it can be seen in some botanic gardens and arboreta growing as a large shrub or small to medium-sized tree to 30 feet (9 m) tall or more. Leaves are medium green, sport rather long petioles up to 1 to 1.25 inches (2.5–3 cm) long, and display little fall foliage color. Flowers are typical for the group, in masses up to 2 inches (5 cm) across with little fragrance. Fruit are 0.25 inch (6 mm) or slightly more in diameter and shiny black but do not last very long.

The bark of *Cornus walteri* is one aspect that sets it apart from others of the group. Young stems are smooth, greenish purple, and rather lustrous. Mature bark on older plants is deeply blocky, reminiscent of *Diospyros virginiana* or alligator hide. A large specimen at the Royal Botanic Gardens, Kew, measures at least 25 feet (7.5 m) tall with a trunk about 12 inches (30 cm) in diameter. While the bark may not sell many plants to the average consumer, barkaphiles seem to be involuntarily attracted to it.

Cornus walteri is native to central China and will grow well in USDA hardiness zones 4 to 8. Some split the Korean (and somewhat larger growing and somewhat less cold hardy form) into its own species as *C. coreana*.

Seed propagation of *Cornus walteri* requires three to five months of cold stratification but is enhanced if preceded by three months of warm stratification. Softwood cuttings treated with 3000 and 8000 ppm IBA rooted 60 percent and 82 percent, respectively.

Cornus walteri (below and below right)

Cornus controversa

CHAPTER 4

THE
Cornus alternifolia
GROUP

THIS GROUP OF OUTSTANDING GARDEN PLANTS has always seemed to play viola to the *Cornus florida*'s lead violin. And while it is true that the members of this clan don't make the same eye-popping splash of their showier cousins, these are without doubt, first-rate garden plants.

As a group, one of the most outstanding features is the architecture. Most members form generally upright oval outlines, but it is the internal structure that stands out. Lateral branches arch gracefully, often upturned at the tips, for an unforgettable look year-round. Add a dusting of snow to the branches and a nice evergreen backdrop, and it is hard to beat.

The floral display can be quite effective, however, since it usually occurs after the leaves emerge; there is not the same spring pizzazz as we are accustomed to with *Cornus florida*. In the *C. alternifolia* group, each inflorescence is a flat-topped cyme with tiny cream-white flowers. The entire display can range from as small as 2 inches (5 cm) or so in diameter to more than 7 inches (17.5 cm) on vigorous specimens of some of the larger growing species.

Culturally, this group has the reputation of being a bit of a prima donna, decidedly un-viola-like. While this reputation does not hold true in every case, members such as *Cornus controversa* 'Variegata', *C. alternifolia* 'Argentea', and a few others have left in their wakes more than a few breathless and red-faced gardeners. But when these dogwoods are well grown, nobody with a pulse would doubt the worthiness of the effort.

Cornus alternifolia

PAGODA DOGWOOD

Cornus alternifolia is in so many ways a bit of a poor cousin to *C. florida* and *C. kousa*, but its subtly delightful characteristics are often overlooked. Properly grown, this singularly beautiful small tree is perfectly at home in the woodland garden or out in open sun.

Growing into a small tree or large, spreading shrub, the plant reaches up to 20 feet (6 m) or so in height and a bit more than that in spread. Branches grow in a wonderful layered arrangement and seem to present the leaves, flowers, and fruit on a platter. While single-stemmed specimens can be effective, multistemmed plants are almost always superior specimens.

As the specific name implies, *Cornus alternifolia* is one of the few members (along with *C. controversa*) of the genus *Cornus* that bears leaves in an alternate arrangement on the stem. Leaves are a deep lustrous green, 2–5 inches (5–12.5 cm) long and half as wide, cuneate and acuminate, with five to seven pairs of veins. Fall foliage can take on a purple to deep reddish hue and can be nice but is seldom spectacular.

While the flowers do not have the show-stopping large white bracts of some flowers of showier relatives, the pagoda dogwood in full flower can be a welcome addition to just about any garden. Individual, creamy white flowers are less than 0.4 inch (9 mm) across, borne in cymes 2–3 inches (5–7.5 cm) across and held above the foliage. They are fairly fragrant as dogwoods go and lend a bit of grace to the late spring and early summer garden. Generally the flowers emerge as the later-blooming viburnums fade, making for a graceful transition into the summer garden.

The fruit is a bluish black drupe, often with a bloomy coating, presented in flat sprays along the branches—rather nice for a black-fruited plant. The birds eventually take the fruit before summer slips away. It has always seemed intriguing that the fruit of these later-flowering dogwoods appears to color earlier in the season than do the fruits of the earlier flowering species.

The young summer stems maintain a glossy greenish purple through the first season or two, changing to a deep glossy wine for the winter. They show prominent, large white to gray lenticels all along the smooth shining bark. Older bark is gray and smooth, eventually developing a shallow ridge and furrow character.

For best growth, *Cornus alternifolia* requires cool, moist conditions and slightly acid soil. It is generally not considered to be a plant for hot, dry summers; however, it has been used quite successfully in much of the upper Midwest. Moisture is the

Cornus alternifolia (above, above right, and below)

key there. Let it dry out once, and it suffers for the rest of the summer. Generally, the species is most at home in areas where soils stay evenly moist, summer soil temperatures stay relatively low, and overhead structure provides a bit of a respite from the hot afternoon summer sun. Who wouldn't be?

In the wilds of the Maine woods, *Cornus alternifolia* often peeks out at the edge of a wood, along wooded roads, or at pond edges. Generally, it remains there, minding its own business for most of the year, only to grab the attention of passersby in June when the flowers emerge.

The native range of the pagoda dogwood runs from eastern Canada, south through the Appalachians and west through much of the Great Plains of the United States. It is best suited to USDA hardiness zones 3–7, though it may suffer in the warmer zone 7 summers of the southeastern United States.

In the garden, this is a fabulous specimen tree, best suited to the woodland garden. While it will take sun with adequate TLC, its architecture loves the woods. While it can be grown as a shrub, to do so is to miss out on its most enduring ornamental feature: that of the exquisite branching. The graceful main trunks weave a wonderful form while the lateral branches are the picture of grace—broadly spreading and delicately upturned at the ends. This is a plant that can serve as a specimen even without the brilliant bracts and bright red fruit of its showier brethren. It works masterfully with an underplanting of ostrich fern or brightly variegated groundcovers. One of the best uses anywhere was a coastal Maine garden with a threesome of *Cornus alternifolia* underplanted with a thick, vigorous mass of *Polygonatum odoratum* 'Variegatum'.

Cornus alternifolia is best produced from seed. Fresh seed harvested and cleaned requires moist stratification for three to five months and then will germinate readily. Cultivars are typically grafted, but it takes a steady and experienced hand to yield anything approaching reasonable success rates. This species can be grafted onto seedling *C. alternifolia* or *C. controversa* rootstock. Softwood cuttings of the species treated with 6000 ppm K-IBA and held under fog can root up to 60 percent. There is no information of this technique having been used on any of the variegated cultivars.

Cornus alternifolia 'Argentea' (synonym 'Variegata'), delicately edged in white, is truly a wonderful selection. It is a bit on the tough side to get going in the garden, some might even label it "performance challenged." But for the devout gardener, it is well worth the effort. 'Argentea' is less treelike than the species and does not seem to be concerned with rapid growth after planting. This grafted selection is not often seen in nurseries in the United States.

Cornus alternifolia **'Corallina'** shows the typical growth for the species, with winter stems of a brighter red.

Cornus alternifolia **'Ochrocarpa'** is the albino of the group. Fruit matures to a yellowish white rather than the typical dark blue-black.

Cornus alternifolia **'Umbraculifera'** has been described in several sources as having conspicuously tiered branches. It is not certain how this distinguishes the cultivar from the species. 'Umbraculifera' is rarely seen.

Cornus alternifolia **'Virescens'** resembles the typical species in all aspects except the greenish new stem growth.

Cornus alternifolia 'Argentea'

Cornus alternifolia **'Wstackman'** (Golden Shadows™) will be a real winner if it lives up to its billing. Large, deep green leaves are set off with a wide chartreuse margin. The plant is supposedly more vigorous than other variegated forms. It was discovered as a branch sport on an unnamed *C. alternifolia* by Walter Stackman of West Chicago, Illinois. Plant patent number PP11,287.

Cornus controversa
WEDDING CAKE TREE, GIANT DOGWOOD

Cornus controversa is a much overlooked, occasionally spectacular species best viewed as the larger, more southerly inclined brother of *C. alternifolia*. Both share the alternate leaf arrangement, tiered branching, and generally wonderful architecture. It's just that *C. controversa* tends to bring these features to new heights; potentially 40 feet (12 m) or more.

Besides being larger overall, *Cornus controversa* tends to be more bold all around. Leaves grow 3–6 inches (7.5–15 cm) long with acuminate apices and acute to cuneate bases. Leaf color is a deep lustrous green, occasionally with purple mixed in, but with little to no fall color. Petioles are long, up to 2 inches (5 cm), resulting in a somewhat pendulous nature to the foliage.

Flowers are mildly fragrant, creamy white, up to 0.5 inch (12 mm) across,

held in cymes above the foliage. The cymes are 4–6 inches (10–15 cm) in diameter. Once again, think *Cornus alternifolia* under the influence of Mark McGuire.

Following the flowers, masses of deep red fruit develop, 0.25 inch (6 mm) in diameter, changing to blue-black. The fruit formed ripens several weeks after those of *Cornus alternifolia*. Stems are more brown than on *C. alternifolia*, with less of the purple and green retained on the second-year stems.

In the culture category, *Cornus controversa* is somewhat enigmatic. Some of Paul's most green-digited gardening friends have thrown in the towel on this species, yet one can occasionally find it growing happily, entirely ignored in its own little world. Certainly one of the major challenges is getting plants through the vagaries of a continental spring. *Cornus controversa*, being an out-of-towner, leafs out a few weeks earlier than the more conservative-minded *C. alternifolia*, the former often experiencing multiple frosty insults from which it rarely recovers. *Cornus controversa* is decidedly more southern minded than *C. alternifolia* though. Less cold tolerant and more heat tolerant, it is at home in USDA hardiness zones 5–7(8).

Cornus controversa is very definitely a specimen plant. It is wonderful as a single lawn tree in open areas. Left to branch to the ground, it can be used as an effective and large-growing summer screen as well.

Cornus controversa (below, below right, and opposite)

Cornus controversa 'Janine' (above and below)

The fruit contains oils that have been used in commercial lubricants and the soap industry. Its dried leaves have been used historically to treat everything from headaches to arthritis and to relieve swelling. Native to Japan, China and the Himalaya, this species was introduced into cultivation around 1880.

***Cornus controversa* 'GrY-C'** is a Japanese selection with yellow new foliage, fading to green as the summer temperatures rise.

***Cornus controversa* 'Hakkouda-no-kagayaki'** ("brightness on the mountain") was originally found in Japan by Kimio Moroya. This selection produces beautiful bright yellow-green leaves in the spring. Through the summer, the leaves gradually go to deeper green in the center.

***Cornus controversa* 'Janine'** originated as a yellow-edged variegated branch sport of an unnamed *C. controversa*. The color is quite pronounced in spring, fading somewhat through the summer. This cultivar was selected by Gary Handy of Handy Nursery, Boring, Oregon.

***Cornus controversa* 'June Snow'** is a very vigorous form selected for good flowering characteristics and rootability.

***Cornus controversa* 'Kansetsu'** ("snow crown") originated as a chance seedling in a Japanese nursery. It has narrow leaves that are splashed with white along the margin and deep green in the center.

***Cornus controversa* 'Marginata Nord'** is listed in the *RHS Plant Finder* as an invalid name.

Cornus controversa **'Pagoda'** is listed but rarely described.

Cornus controversa **'Pk-Mg'** is a striking Japanese cultivar with bright pink-red leaf edges and light green in the center. The leaves are narrow and sharp pointed. This selection may very well have been lost to cultivation.

Cornus controversa **'Rag Doll'** is rarely listed and without description.

Cornus controversa **'Variegata'** is a singularly gorgeous tree with wide, irregular white-edged variegation. The layered effect of the branches is truly spectacular when backed by a good bank of dark evergreens. While this cultivar is a bit easier to grow than *C. alternifolia* 'Argentea', one would be best to prepare for disappointment. Paul has tried to grow it on the coast of Maine, in southern New York, and in north-central Kentucky. In all three sites he has watched no fewer than three specimens unmercifully thrashed by late spring freezes (or was it premature spring bud break?). Is he still trying? You bet. Krüssman (1984) listed this as introduced in 1896 by Barbier.

Cornus controversa 'June Snow'

Cornus controversa 'Variegata'

Cornus controversa '**Variegata Frans Type**' resembles *C. controversa* 'Variegata' with the white variegation narrower, the green foliage portion grayer, and the constitution a bit sturdier. This selection originated in northern France but has failed to make much noise in the United States. Considering the Herculean efforts worldwide by frustrated gardeners trying to successfully grow the former, one would think the French selection would garner a bit more attention. Maybe Paul will try this one next.

Cornus controversa 'Variegata', at Trewithen Gardens, Cornwall, United Kingdom

Cornus macrophylla

BIGLEAF DOGWOOD

Cornus macrophylla is a large and variable species, producing mature plants from 25 to 75 feet (7.5–22.5 m) tall depending on seed source and cultural conditions. In the more moist and kindly sections of its native habitat throughout much of central and southern China (and reportedly all the way to Afghanistan and Pakistan), the tree can reach its greatest size. In his 1894 *Forest Flora of Japan*, Charles Sargent reported finding the species primarily between 4000 and 8000 feet (1200–2400 m) elevation in China and Korea. He reported it to be the largest member of the genus, reaching 50–60 feet (15 m) in the wild. In gardens, it typically won't go much beyond 35–40 feet (10.5–12 m), but even at this size, it is clearly one of the largest of the group.

Specimens of this species are broadly rounded plants, often multitrunked, and of reasonably regular outline. In full sun, branching is layered and foliage can be quite dense. In shade, and it can take a fair amount of shade, the branch layering is more open and sculptural. (Paul's plant materials students always accused him of using the adjective "sculptural" for plants he liked and "scraggly" for those he didn't. He always suggested they grow the plant and decide for themselves.) Either sun or shade, the plant has a pleasant structure at all points of the calendar.

The flat green, opposite leaves are large, reaching up to 7 inches (17.5 cm) long and 3 inches (7.5 cm) wide with a rounded base and an acuminate apex. The gray-green below offers a slight two-toned look in a gentle breeze. Fall color is a muted red to yellow and is not one of the best traits of this otherwise serviceable plant. While some confuse this species in youth with *Cornus alternifolia* and *C. controversa*, *C. macrophylla* is easily picked out by virtue of its opposite leaves.

The creamy white flowers, 0.5 inch (12 mm) across, are arranged in flattened panicles up to 6 inches (15 cm) in diameter and are borne from late spring through midsummer depending on the seed source. The individual flowers are more widely spaced, in almost a lacelike arrangement compared to those of *Cornus controversa* and *C. alternifolia*. In fact the venerable plant hunter Frank Kingdon-Ward wrote of the effect of a tree in flower, "the flat leafy limbs look as though lace had been laid over them." 'Nough said.

The fruit is a drupe, 0.25 inch (6 mm) in diameter and blackish, ripening in late summer but not persisting very long. Stems are purplish or yellow in new stem growth soon turning smooth gray.

Cornus macrophylla is one of the easiest of the tree dogwoods to grow. It prefers moist, well-drained soil, but then again, what plant doesn't? It will adapt nicely to dry sites once established. One plant at Bernheim Arboretum, Clermont, Kentucky, is situated on a very dry hillside on clay soil in heavy shade. The plant flowers sparsely but has been in the ground for more than 15 years and is easily as many feet (4.5 m) tall. The species transplants readily. Summer stem cuttings root reasonably well. The plant performs well in sun or shade from USDA hardiness zones 5 to 7. Are we missing something here? Why is this plant not in cultivation in a larger way? It is useful as a single specimen, a small grove, or even a small street tree. This tremendously versatile plant deserves a great deal more attention. With this kind of adaptability and native populations into India and Afghanistan, is there some potential here for a smallish southern street tree? One would think so.

This dogwood has great potential for the landscape. It has been all but entirely overlooked by the horticultural profession and gardening public. Given the plant's adaptability and ornamental appeal, the smart nursery professional might want to start bulking up and doing some selection work.

There are no commercially available cultivars on the market today; however,

Cornus macrophylla (below and below right)

taxonomists commonly identify two distinct varieties. *Cornus macrophylla* var. *macrophylla* is the typical species while *C. macrophylla* var. *stracheyi* shows a more heavily pubescent inflorescence—not that a pubescent inflorescence would make any difference in a garden. Variety *stracheyi* also bears slightly smaller individual flowers about two to three weeks later than those of the typical variety, and its fruit is slightly smaller than that of the type.

Seed propagation requires three to five months of cold stratification. Softwood cuttings root quite readily when treated with 3000 to 8000 ppm IBA.

Cornus florida 'Purple Glory'

CHAPTER 5

THE
Cornus florida
GROUP

IN WRITING A BOOK ON SUCH AS THIS, one is tugged to constantly engage in superlative one-upmanship. We have done our best to temper some of our enthusiasm throughout, although one might not recognize that in the resulting pages; however, if you cannot pull out the cork of superlative overuse for a group like this, we don't know when you would.

A diverse and widespread group of species, this assemblage represents some of the most spectacular of the flowering trees offered to gardeners. And while we are all quite taken with the searing fall foliage color, brilliant scarlet fruit, and winter branching structure, it is the spring florals that have made the name for the dogwoods. It is ironic that among the most famous and recognizable of all flowering trees, this clan attributes its display not to the floral petals, but from greatly expanded bracts. But honestly, who cares; bracts schmacts. To most of the world they are flowers, thank you very much.

The variation in the *Cornus florida* group runs from deciduous to evergreen, white to yellow to pink floral displays, and intolerably astringent to surprisingly palatable. Is it too much of a cliché to say that every garden should have at least one?

Cornus florida
FLOWERING DOGWOOD

Cornus florida is the pinnacle to which most other species covered here have been compared. And you've finally made it (assuming you did not skip ahead to get to the "good part"—and shame on you if you have)! Few plants of the Northern Hemisphere are equally rivaled and as instantly recognizable. Ok, the rose probably wins in that category, but who can compete there? But here's a question: If there was no *C. florida* to write about, would there be much demand for a book on dogwoods? Maybe, and maybe not.

Still, where would most of suburban, mid-temperate North America be without the flowering dogwood? Choose just about any typical subdivision in the eastern half of the continent between Birmingham (Alabama) and Chicago (Illinois) across to Boston (Massachusetts) and through much of the Pacific Northwest, and fully half the small flowering trees are *Cornus florida*. In some places, they can account for nearly all such plantings. The white spring bracts with a peppering of pink forms all but fully describe the Rockwellian landscape. Want to look at it another way? Consider that the Tennessee wholesale dogwood crop alone is worth more than $50 million!

For those who have spent most of their life in Atlantis and thus may not be familiar with the species, flowering dogwood forms a small to medium tree up to 25 feet (7.5 m), occasionally as tall as 40 feet (12 m) or more. Young plants tend to be upright to rounded with large old specimens growing up to 50 percent wider than tall. The lateral branches are strongly horizontal and form an instantly recognizable character in the winter landscape.

The leaves are 3–6 inches (7.5–15 cm) long and half as wide, acuminate, cuneate or rounded at the base, medium green above and lighter below with minute gray hairs on veins beneath. Fall color can be a spectacular red to purple as long as the leaves make it through the summer in good condition.

The true flowers are typically 0.25–0.4 inch (6–9 mm) in diameter, yellow to green, and borne in umbels that are 0.75 inch (2 cm) in diameter. They are rarely fragrant. Of course, the showy part of the inflorescence is the set of four bracts that cover the true flowers through the winter. Bracts vary from rounded to narrow-ovate with the entire display ranging from 3 to 5 inches (7.5–12.5 cm) across. Bracts may be clear white, creamy, pink to nearly red. Some have a noticeable cleft at the apex.

Of course, the legend of the dogwood flower is that its wood was used to fashion the cross on which Christ was crucified. It seems the dogwood once grew as tall as the oak and other noble trees of the forest, but the shame of being used in the crucifixion caused the dogwood great distress and sadness. Recognizing the dogwood's pain, Jesus is said to have promised to render the tree forevermore unsuited for such a use. From that point on, the tree was to be bent and twisted so the wood would be unsuitable for any use that required a straight length. Further-

Cornus florida

more, the petals were to be borne in the shape of a cross, with a rusty red nail mark at the tip of each and a crown of thorns in the center of the blossom. Of course, given that *Cornus florida* doesn't grow within 2000 miles (3200 km) of Golgotha, the site where Christ was crucified, does make this story a bit of a stretch, but it certainly helps one to remember the characteristics just the same.

Fruit is a brilliant red, shiny drupe 0.5 inch (12 mm) long and 0.3 inch (8 mm) wide, borne in groups of as few as 1 or 2 and as many as 10 or more. Red coloration develops in late summer and then the party begins. Dozens of bird species dine on the fruits, but some fruits may remain on the plant into winter where they add nicely to a dusting of snow or a coating of ice. Yellow-fruited forms are found occasionally, often with a red blush, not unlike a Golden Delicious apple. The common name of dogwood comes from one colonial description of the fruit as being technically edible but not fit for a dog! The hard stone in each fruit is roughly the trait for which the genus was named. *Cornus* ("horn") refers to the hardness of the seed coat. Of course, this same linguistic attribute is often related about the hardness of the wood.

Young stems are purple to reddish green the first year, turning gray by year two. Older branches and trunks develop a wonderful blocky pattern of dark gray. The wood is incredibly dense but highly susceptible to decay.

Cultural management is the bane of the flowering dogwood's existence. The tree does best in moist, acidic soil in a site with a touch of afternoon shade. It will perform admirably in full sun with adequate moisture, but who can be trusted to provide adequate water? Can you just hear it now, "I promise, honey, I'll water it twice a week . . . !"

Certainly the most significant suburban malady of the flowering dogwood is mower blight. The constant insult to the trunk from overzealous weekend lawn warriors seems to almost insure the extinction of the species. One nick here. Another there. Soon the borers march in, the borers march out. 'Nough said!

Cornus florida has tremendously dense and hard wood with a very tight grain. Fortunately for the wood splitter, the tree rarely reaches adequate size to require the procedure. The wood has been used for mallets, wooden rake teeth, jeweler's boxes, butcher's blocks, and anything else requiring extremely durable and dense wood.

Unfortunately, the density of the wood does not impart a resistance to decay. Flowering dogwoods abhor large pruning cuts. Bark damage of any kind heals very slowly, allowing ample time and opportunity to all manner of nasties.

Seed propagation of *Cornus florida* is straightforward and forms the basis of the entire flowering dogwood cultivar market. Seeds are sown in fall into prepared

Cornus florida (above, above right, below, below right)

rows, then covered with sawdust or sand; they emerge the following spring. Clean seed that has been cold stratified for 90 to 120 days germinates near 100 percent. Softwood cuttings treated with 8,000 to 10,000 ppm IBA can root between 50 and 85 percent if the timing is just right. This technique, however, has remained on the sidelines as budding continues to be the method of choice for growers. The same holds true for tissue culture propagation. Rooted cuttings should remain undisturbed through the dormant season to achieve maximum success.

Cornus florida **'Abundance',** as the name implies, produces profuse masses of large-bracted white displays. It is a vigorous grower that begins life upright but, like most of us, spreads with age. It is similar in look and maybe identity to 'Cloud 9'.

Cornus florida **'Alba Plena'** displays double bracts (six to eight per inflorescence) at the end of each branch that come together to make a delightful show. As doubles go, this selection flowers quite heavily but the best show is up close.

Cornus florida **'American Beauty'** produces deep red bracts that fade to white at the base to give a bit of a white-eye effect to the overall display. Leaves are dark, glossy green with a bit of purple pigmentation. Don believes that 'American Beauty' is very likely the same as 'Sweetwater Red'.

Cornus florida **'Amerika Touch-O-Pink'** is described as having larger-than-normal leaves, bract displays up to 6 inches (15 cm) across, and good disease resistance. Bracts are tinged pink along the margin. This cultivar was selected by Howard W. Stanley of Reidsville, Georgia, from Georgia coastal plain seed. Plant patent number PP10,423.

Cornus florida **'Andrea Hart'** is smaller and more densely branched than most *C. florida* cultivars. It likely won't grow taller than 6–8 feet (1.8–2.4 m), and it has medium pink bracts. This selection is occasionally listed as 'Andy Heart'.

Cornus florida **'Angel Wings',** a large, white-bracted form selected by Webb of Huntsville, Alabama, is not widely distributed.

Cornus florida **'Appalachian Spring',** introduced by the University of Tennessee, shows a great abundance of flowers with fairly large white bracts that do not overlap. This upright selection has dark green foliage that develops good red fall foliage color. In a USDA Forest Service screening study, this cultivar demonstrated superior resistance to dogwood anthracnose. While the cultivar showed some foliar lesions, it was the only plant to survive the screening. The original plant was discovered as a lone survivor from a population growing in Catoctin National Mountain Park, Maryland. All other *C. florida* specimens in the area had been either killed or severely damaged by dogwood anthracnose.

Cornus florida **'Apple Blossom'** has medium-sized bracts with light pink, especially toward the apex and margin of each bract. The original plant was discovered in New Canaan, Connecticut, and was first offered by Wayside Gardens of Mentor, Ohio, along with 'Spring Song'.

Cornus florida **'Ascending'** was patented in 1952 as an upright growing variety. According to Wyman (1967), it is nearly identical to 'Fastigiata'.

Cornus florida **'Aurea'** produces brilliant yellow-gold leaves that last through the spring but tend to burn a bit by midsummer in Kentucky. This cultivar is somewhat susceptible to spot anthracnose. It is probably best in a bit of afternoon shade in warmer areas.

Cornus florida **'Autumn Gold'** was selected and named by Don from a group of seedlings originally grown and selected for bright yellow and orange stems, by

Cornus florida 'Autumn Gold' (below and below right)

Manuel Statham of Commercial Nursery Company, Decherd, Tennessee. It has wide white bracts, bright red fruit, gold fall color, and yellow and orange winter twigs.

Cornus florida **'Barton'** was named by Marvin Barton of Birmingham, Alabama, for his introduction of a precocious flowering, vigorous plant with broad clear white bracts. The selection was quite resistant to stem canker and moderately susceptible to spot anthracnose. A North Carolina State University report indicated 'Barton' to be highly resistant to powdery mildew. The cultivar was quite similar in characteristics to 'Cloud 9' but was originally a distinct selection. Molecular work done at the University of Tennessee seems to indicate that the material now in the trade under this name is most often identical to 'Cloud 9'.

Cornus florida **'Belmont Pink'**, a pale pink-bracted form, was supposedly discovered by Henry Hicks at or near Belmont race track in New York around 1930. It is not currently known in cultivation.

Cornus florida **'Big Bouquet'**, a compact plant with large masses of broad white bracts, was introduced by Vermeulen Nursery, Neshanic Station, New Jersey.

Cornus florida **'Big Giant'** has been described in some references as a selection with large white bracts on a broad-spreading tree. If ever it was, this may no longer represent a distinct offering.

Cornus florida **'Big Girl'** supposedly is a large-bracted form, but as with 'Big Giant', this may no longer exist in commerce.

Cornus florida **'Blonde Luster'** has yellow-green to chartreuse foliage and is thus relegated to sites in partial shade in warmer cli-

Cornus florida 'Barton'

Cornus florida 'Blonde Luster'

mates. In full shade it goes partially green, and in full sun it burns a bit. The bracts are broad and deeply ridged. In good years, if the foliage stays in good shape through the summer, fall color can be a beautiful mix of yellow, orange, and a touch of red. 'Blonde Luster' is surprisingly vigorous for an off-green selection. It has been sometimes listed as a cultivar of *C. kousa*.

***Cornus florida* 'Bonnie'** was introduced by Louisiana State University and described as producing bract displays 6 inches (15 cm) in diameter and bright red fruit. While 6 inches might be a bit optimistic, the cultivar does make a bold display. This selection has a low chill requirement so may be most useful in the southern United States.

***Cornus florida* 'Cherokee Chief'** has good deep red bracts, the color of which can vary tremendously depending on sun exposure. A strong grower, this selection produces reddish new growth and uniform branching. It has shown moderate mildew resistance. 'Cherokee Chief' was introduced in 1958 by Ike Hawkersmith of Winchester, Tennessee. It was selected by Howell Nursery, Sweetwater, Tennessee, from a group of 'Prosser Red' seedlings grown at the nursery. The plant was originally grown and sold under the name 'Super Red' by some Tennessee nurserymen before it was patented under the 'Cherokee Chief' name. It is a sister seedling to 'Sweetwater Red'.

Some confusion exists between this form and the similar 'Royal Red'. Elwin Orton (pers. comm.) related that one day he and his technician vowed to check

Cornus florida 'Cherokee Chief'

Cornus florida 'Royal Red'

the similarity. *Cornus florida* is quite variable in the number of flowers per inflorescence, but on a single tree (or a single cultivar—clone) they are quite consistent. Orton and his technician decided to count the number of flowers on 100 blossoms of each cultivar. The result—2301 for 'Cherokee Chief' and 2304 for 'Royal Red'. You connect the dots. Plant patent number PP1,710.

***Cornus florida* 'Cherokee Maiden',** a name that has occasionally popped up in reference to 'Ozark Spring', a selection of the late John Pair of Kansas State University, does not appear to be a valid name.

***Cornus florida* 'Cherokee Princess'** is not as cold hardy as 'Ozark Spring' but is a close second. It produces a large, white bract display, 5 inches (12.5 cm) in diameter, on a broad-spreading and dense plant. This dogwood has shown reasonable resistance to powdery mildew, spot anthracnose, and stem canker in several tests. It was discovered and named by W. C. Higden of Mayfield, Kentucky, and introduced in 1959 by Ike Hawkersmith in Winchester, Tennessee, as 'Sno-White'. In 1963 it was registered as 'Cherokee Princess'.

Cornus florida 'Cherokee Princess'

Cornus florida **'Clear Moon'** is listed without description by a couple of European plant nurseries.

Cornus florida **'Cloud 9'** was introduced in 1951 by Henry Chase, Chase Nursery, Alabama, as a form that reliably flowers heavily as a young plant. John Pair, Kansas State University, ranked this as one of the most cold hardy forms. According to the folks at the University of Tennessee Dogwood Research Group (Witte et al. 2000), this cultivar is among the least bothered by canker. Although it shows some susceptibility to spot anthracnose, it is reasonably resistant to powdery mildew. Overall, 'Cloud 9' is a reliable, heavily flowered form with wide, overlapping white bracts. It has performed admirably in many study plantings, although it is somewhat slower growing than many others. According to molecular work done at the University of Tennessee (Witte et al. 2000), 'Cloud 9' is identical to what is now sold as 'Barton'. Initially distinct selections, they somehow got confused in the trade. Plant patent number PP2,112.

Cornus florida '**Cochise',** a pink form selected by Webb of Huntsville, Alabama, is likely not in circulation any longer.

Cornus florida **'Comco No. 1'** (Cherokee Brave™), one of the better mildew-resistant forms, has pink bract displays with a pale pink or white center. A touch of red appears in the newly emerging leaves. Discovered by Manual Statham and Hubert Nicholson, this cultivar was introduced by Commercial Nursery Company, Decherd, Tennessee. It is assumed to have arisen as a seedling of 'Cherokee Chief'. Plant patent number PP10,166.

Cornus florida 'Comco No. 1'

Cornus florida **'Compacta',** a name that has become one of many taxonomic dumping grounds in the world of *Cornus* nomenclutter, serves generally for seedling forms showing short internodes and overall small stature.

Cornus florida **'Daniela'** was selected by Mr. Gilardelli of Milan, Italy, and named by him for one of his daughters. This yellow and green variegated form has not been thoroughly tested in the United States.

Cornus florida **'Daybreak'** (Cherokee Daybreak™), a green-leaved, white-edged form, was discovered as a seedling variant. Several successive propagation cycles were required to finally produce the stable form available today. This selection holds up well in full sun with little scorching but occasionally shows some fairly heavy powdery mildew. It is an upright, vigorous grower with white bracts and good red fall foliage color. It was introduced by Commercial Nursery Company, Decherd, Tennessee. Plant patent number PP6,320.

Cornus florida **'De Kalb Red'** has purple-red bracts similar in color to 'Purple Glory' but less twisted. This slow grower averages 6–10 inches (15–25 cm) of shoot growth per year. It was named for the De Kalb Nursery in Norristown, Pennsylvania.

Cornus florida **'Dixie Collonade'** was discovered by Don in northern Alabama. The original plant was 22 feet (6.6 m) tall and not more than 8 feet (2.4 m) wide, more or less the same width bottom to top.

Cornus florida **'Dunnewell'** is listed in several places without description.

Cornus florida **'Eternal Dogwood',** a double white selection with 12 to 20 bracts, was discovered in the 1990s by Pierre W. Simmen at his residence in Davidson County, North Carolina. While it is sometimes listed as 'Eternal', the correct patented cultivar name is 'Eternal Dogwood'. Plant patent number PP13,069.

Cornus florida **'Fastigiata'** has an upright form and is quite distinct as a young plant. With age, the lateral branches begin to spread; however, the ascending nature of the main trunks continues to hint of the youthful tendencies. Eventually, the tree grows twice as tall as wide. Bracts are typical for the species. The original tree grew at the Arnold Arboretum from 1910 and was distributed to 15 nurseries in 1954.

Cornus florida **'Fayetteville Columnar'** is listed by Dirr (1998) as a slow-growing form, not particularly columnar.

Cornus florida **'First Lady'** is the ideal dogwood if one is in the market for a screamer in the landscape. Leaves are dark green in the center with irregular marginal blotches of brilliant gold to chartreuse. The plant makes an excellent specimen for brightening a dark corner in the garden, although too much shade will see

Cornus florida 'Daybreak' (above and above right)

Cornus florida 'First Lady' (below and below right)

the leaves go almost all green in summer. Fading is more pronounced in the more southern end of the plant's range. 'First Lady' is among the few variegated forms that stands the test of near full sun in Kentucky landscapes. Bracts are white but are not borne in large quantities. The plant is susceptible to mildew but reasonably resistant to spot anthracnose and canker. One of the best specimens grows in Cave Hill Cemetery, Louisville, Kentucky. This selection was introduced in 1969 by the Boyd Nursery Company, McMinnville, Tennessee. Plant patent number PP2,916.

***Cornus florida* 'Flower Chief',** an early selection of Webb of Huntsville, Alabama, likely no longer survives as a distinct cultivar.

Cornus florida 'Fragrant Cloud' (below and below right)

***Cornus florida* 'Fragrant Cloud'** reportedly emits a sweet perfume when in flower. Paul admits that he gets at best a faint whiff that is lost if he moves more than 10 feet (3 m) away. Of course, when it comes to olfactory prowess, Paul does not excel. The cultivar shows some susceptibility to canker, but it is rarely a significant prob-

lem. It is also fairly resistant to spot anthracnose. The original plant was found on the grounds of the Buckhorn Inn in Gatlinburg, Tennessee, in 1968 and was introduced by Henry Chase of Chase Nursery in Alabama.

Cornus florida **'Geronimo'** is occasionally listed but rarely encountered. It was selected by Webb of Huntsville, Alabama, for bright red new stem growth. Harald Neubauer of Belvidere, Tennessee, has grown several seedlings with red twig growth but none are named as of this writing.

Cornus florida **'Gigantea'** was discovered in 1932 on the famed Phipps estate of Long Island, New York, by Paul Vossburg of the Westbury Rose Company, Westbury, New York. The plant produces bract displays reportedly 6 inches (15 cm) from tip to tip.

Cornus florida **'Gold Braid',** discovered by Jimmy Leland of Gainous' Shade Tree Nursery in Cairo, Georgia, shows vigorous growth to a pyramidal form, and yellow variegation. The selection supposedly resists foliage burn in the southern United States and is reasonably resistant to spot anthracnose. White bracts are sparsely produced. Plant patent number PP13,085.

Cornus florida **'Golden Nugget',** an edge-variegated form with medium green center and marginal golden-yellow markings, is not as bright as 'First Lady'. It tends to brown a bit in full sun and go all green in heavy shade. Several reports indicate this to be a rather vigorous form for a variegated cultivar. It is occasionally listed as 'Gold Nugget'.

Cornus florida **'Green Glow'** originated as a sport of 'Welchii' with a light green irregular central portion on a field of deep, emerald green. It is one of the most vigorous forms, heavy flowering, and upright in branching. It also has good dark red fall foliage color. 'Green Glow' was introduced by Glen Handy, Troutdale, Oregon, and patented in 1979. Plant patent number PP4,444.

Cornus florida **'Heistar'** is occasionally listed but no information is available.

Cornus florida **'Hillenmeyer'** is a precocious-flowering form that produces tremendous masses of white. It is among the early "improved" white selections offered, having been grown since the 1950s at least. It is occasionally listed under 'Hillenmeyer White'.

***Cornus florida* 'Hohman's Golden',** with foliage of medium green over yellow green, is an enticing selection that puts on quite a display in spring, summer, and fall. Fall color is a mélange from dark red to almost pink. A striking group of specimens used to grow in the garden of Bill and Nancy Frederick of Hockessin, Delaware. The bullfrog statue, 6 feet (1.8 m) tall, that sat beside the trees was truly a sight to behold. Introduced from Wayne, New Jersey, in 1964, this cultivar was named in honor of Henry J. Hohman, founder of Kingsville Nursery in Maryland.

Cornus florida 'Hohman's Golden'

Cornus florida **'Imperial White',** a North Carolina selection, was described as having large white bract displays up to 6 inches (15 cm) in diameter, broad vigorous growth, larger-than-normal leaves, and improved drought tolerance. The name may no longer represent an extant taxon. The original plant was discovered in 1975 by Elizabeth Parris Blow and Muriel Fiscus Steppe in the former's boxwood garden in Raleigh, North Carolina. Plant patent number PP4,242.

Cornus florida **'Irving Cline'** is rarely listed and without description.

Cornus florida **'Jean's Appalachian Snow'** is probably the best of the new powdery mildew resistant introductions from the Tennessee Agricultural Experiment Station. It flowers heavily as a young plant to produce large overlapping, wide white bracts that can be a little floppy. The flower petals have a distinct green tinge compared to the yellow typical of the species. Plant patent number PP13,099.

Cornus florida **'Jessica's Bouquet'** was found by Gary Lanham of Lebanon, Kentucky, as a branch sport on a large tree. According to Lanham (pers. comm.), the original sport produced as many as 100 blossoms in a square foot (900 sq cm). Paul, who has seen the sport (unfortunately not in flower at the time), would not argue. Grafted plants have been slow growing and slow to set buds. Compared to 'Pygmy', 'Jessica's Bouquet' is slower growing and produces smaller bracts. Unfortunately, grafts have proven to be a bit brittle. This cultivar was named for Lanham's granddaughter who was tragically killed after being hit by a car when going to the mailbox one afternoon.

Cornus florida 'Jessica's Bouquet'

Cornus florida 'Juanita'

Cornus florida **'Juanita',** selected by Paul, was found as a chance seedling growing in the yard of Juanita and Jim McKinney, Louisville, Kentucky. Enormous bract displays measure more than 5 inches (12.5 cm) across (yes, Paul has actually measured them, not just estimated like most!) on a plant that has proven to be fairly resistant to powdery mildew.

Cornus florida 'Juanita'

***Cornus florida* 'Junior Miss Variegated',** a variegated sport of 'Welch's Junior Miss', was discovered and introduced by Akiri Shibamichi of Japan. Cream, green, and pink combine for a striking display of this pink-bracted form. Some reports indicate that stability of the variegation may be a problem. The plant is a weak grower.

***Cornus florida* 'Karen's Appalachian Blush',** one of several new introductions from the Tennessee Agricultural Experiment Station, was selected for resistance to powdery mildew. Bract displays are broad, flat, separate, and delicate, edged in a touch of pink. Bracts do not overlap. While this dogwood was originally described as being highly resistant to powdery mildew, young plants have shown some mildew in subsequent seasons. Plant patent number PP13,165.

***Cornus florida* 'Kay's Appalachian Mist',** another of the Tennessee Agricultural Experiment Station selections, shows good resistance to mildew. This form has large, stiff, ribbed, slightly overlapping creamy white bracts with a prominent cleft at the tip. The tree is a somewhat precocious bloomer and produces nice red fall foliage. Plant patent number PP13,098.

***Cornus florida* 'Kingsville Form',** selected by Henry J. Hohman, Kingsville Nursery, Maryland, was described as similar to 'Welchii' but having stronger coloration and exhibiting better growth. Apparently it was not widely distributed. It is identical to 'Aureo-variegata' and was listed by Brimfield Nursery, Wethersfield, Connecticut, in 1958.

***Cornus florida* 'Lanham's Little Broom'** is one of the smallest and tightest cultivars out there. It originated as a branch sport and was discovered by Gary Lanham of Lebanon, Kentucky. A five-year-old plant from a bud was less than 3 feet (90 cm) tall and 2 feet (60 cm) wide with densely set foliage. Flowering is somewhat sparse.

***Cornus florida* 'Lemon Drops'** bears generous crops of broad white, deeply ribbed bracts on young plants. Leaves are a bit

Cornus florida 'Lanham's Little Broom'

Cornus florida 'Lemon Drops' (above and below)

wavy along the margin and have yellow variegation that can cover more than half the leaf blade. The variegation shows up as the leaves mature and then only on plants that receive sufficient sun. Plants grown in full shade develop no variegation. Fruit is red. 'Lemon Drops' was selected by Rick Dillworth of Dillworth Nursery, Oxford, Pennsylvania.

Cornus florida **'Little Princess'** was selected and introduced by Don. This sport of 'Cherokee Princess' is of modest growth, falling somewhere between typical *Cornus florida* and 'Pygmy'. It blooms nicely as a young plant.

Cornus florida **'Magnifica',** a Long Island selection with large floral bract displays over 4 inches (10 cm) in diameter, is similar to 'Gigantea'.

Cornus florida **'Mary Ellen'** produces sparse double-bracted displays. It is a nice form up close, but not overwhelming at a distance. Bob MacDonald of the University of Tennessee Arboretum introduced this cultivar around 1966.

Cornus florida **'Miss Marion',** selected and introduced by Bill Craven of Twisted Oaks Nursery in Waynesboro, Georgia, is a white, double-bracted form.

Cornus florida **'Montpelier',** a double-bracted form from New England apparently selected by a Gary Perrygo of the Maryland National Park Planning Commission, is not likely still in production.

Cornus florida **'Moon'** produces tremendous masses of flowers bearing large, broad bracts. This selection yields a unique texture in the landscape when in flower.

Cornus florida **'Moonglow'** (synonym 'Chiaro Di Luna') may have originally had an Italian or English name. No one seems to know. The description here comes from Karan Junker of PMA Plant Specialties, Taunton, Somerset, United Kingdom. (This plant is included here to give the reader a glimpse into the silliness that can sometimes surround ornamental plant nomenclature.)

> Moonglow, we got from Italy. Having checked my records, I see that it was originally labeled 'Chiaro Di Luna'. Why we call it by the translation I do not remember. If it was named in Italy, then my opinion is that it should be known by the Italian name, not anglicized. What I'm now not sure of is whether the Italian version was itself a translation of the original . . . I

don't know where it actually originated. Anyway, it is most similar to 'Golden Nugget'—that is, upright habit, (though not as much so as 'Golden Nugget'—but definitely not the arching form of 'First Lady'), golden foliage, white flowers, but shy flowering (unless that is my conditions—too shady perhaps?).

Cornus florida **'Mr. Theodore'** has large, glossy leaves that show considerable resistance to powdery mildew. The plant was discovered by Theodore Klein, Crestwood, Kentucky, on the grounds of the Sleepy Hollow golf course. The cultivar name comes from Mike Hayman of Louisville, Kentucky.

Cornus florida **'Multibracteata'** is a name of utter nomenclatural nonsense!

Cornus florida **'Mystery'** is a compact form with white bracts showing occasional dark pink spots. Reports indicate it to be fairly drought tolerant, but we are always suspicious of such claims. A drought-tolerant *C. florida* is like a lightening-tolerant golfer. The plant has some resistance to powdery mildew. This selection was introduced by Jim Carson of Winchester, Tennessee, through a patent application written by nurseryman Fred Galle around 1965. When asked why he called it 'Mystery', Carson simply stated, "It's a mystery why it occurred in my block of seedlings."

Cornus florida **'New Hampshire',** a cold-hardy form selected in Atkinson, New Hampshire, by Heinrich Rohrbach of Heatherfells Nursery, Andover, Massachusetts, may no longer exist in cultivation.

Cornus florida **'October Glory'** is a pink-bracted form that has been successfully produced by cutting. It has excellent red fall color. It was introduced by Princeton Nurseries, Allentown, New Jersey.

Cornus florida 'Ozark Spring'

Cornus florida **'Ozark Spring'** is a clean white-bracted, free-growing form selected by John Pair of Kansas State University. It is a reliably cold-tolerant form with flower buds surviving −22 to −24°F (−30 to −31°C) in lab studies and in Kansas field tests, out-performing 'Cherokee Princess' and several other fine

Cornus florida 'Ozark Spring'

selections. 'Ozark Spring' originated from seed collected in the Cherokee Mountains of northern Oklahoma. As it was seedling number KS-75-66 in Pair's trials, the name '66' has been incorrectly tied to this cultivar.

***Cornus florida* 'Pacific Gold'** is presumably a gold-leafed selection. The one plant Paul saw was covered with powdery mildew.

***Cornus florida* 'Pendula'** is the moniker under which numerous forms, some with weeping tendencies, are sold. Most of these plants form lumpy haystacks with somewhat twisted bracts and leaves and are about as easy to use well in the landscape as a '75 Dodge Dart up on blocks! The plants are interesting as specimens in the right spots. One form was introduced under this name by the Meehan Nursery of Philadelphia, Pennsylvania, in the late 1800s.

Cornus florida 'Pendula'

Cornus florida **'Peve Rhoode'**, a Dutch selection, presumably has pink bracts.

Cornus florida **'Phillips Pink No. 1'** is a double form with up to eight medium pink, somewhat wavy bracts. Bloom is quite heavy and late compared to that of other *C. florida* selections, as is the case for most doubles. The plant was discovered by Walter Phillips on his farm near Frankford, Delaware, and patented in 1993. Plant patent number PP8,518.

Cornus florida **'Pink Autumn'**, an Oregon sport, produces deep pink bracts followed by reddish spring foliage that matures to a subtle variegation of creamy yellow. It is not a good selection for the thermally enhanced! The foliage burns in full sun in the southeastern United States.

Cornus florida **'Pink Blush'** produces pale pink bracts on a medium-sized tree with slight tinges of red in the new foliage.

Cornus florida **'Pink Flame'** was introduced to the trade by Mel Wills of Fairview, Oregon, a field grafter for Handy Nursery. It was discovered as a branch sport of *C. florida* 'Welchii' but is much improved; it is faster, sturdier, and stronger in growth habit. Where 'Welchii' is greenish white and pink in leaf, 'Pink Flame' is more green, yellow, and pink. Bracts are of a medium pink. This selection has shown excellent heat tolerance in North Carolina and California evaluations. Plant patent number PP4,300.

Cornus florida **'Pink Princess'**, a 1988-patented form, bears medium pink bracts and large, flat, smooth leaves with deep green centers and white margins. Compared to *C. florida* 'Wills', 'Pink Princess' is more upright and has larger leaves with a more pronounced white margin and less ruffling to the leaf edge. The original plant was discovered on the grounds of the Perkins DeWilde Nursery of Shiloh, New Jersey, by John C. Lowery, Monkton, Maryland, and Matthew J. Wingle of Augusta, New Jersey. Plant patent number PP6,195.

Cornus florida **'Pink Sachet'** produces rich pink, full bracts with bronzy new foliage. It was selected for its floral fragrance described in the original plant patent document as "generally resembling the composite fragrance of gardenia, honeysuckle, and calycanthus." The fragrance may be noticeable up close, but don't look to the fragrance of this one to pull in passersby off the street. The original plant was found growing among a block of *C. florida* 'Cherokee Chief' plants on the property of Wayside Nurseries at Raleigh, North Carolina. The original description states that "since the plant was located in a bed which had been treated with radioactive phosphorus approximately 10 years earlier, it is believed that the modification . . . may have come about as a genetic change due to radioactivity." Quite a story indeed! 'Pink Sachet' was selected and introduced by Clarence M. Steppe, Raleigh, North Carolina. Plant patent number PP3,993.

***Cornus florida* 'Plena'** is of uncertain origin. We have done our best to track down the origin of this taxon, but its history seems to have gone the way of the dodo. In various collections, Paul studied and photographed so-named specimens with 6 to 13 bracts, some full and broad, others twisted and barely there. Some are quite nice. Most flower a week or two after typical *C. florida*. The name seems to be a taxonomic dumping ground for multibracted forms of questionable lineage, most being sterile. In the University of Tennessee Agricultural Extension Service bulletin *Dogwoods for American Gardens* (Witte et al. 2000), the authors list 'Plena' as being immune to spot anthracnose. It would be nice to know which "Plena" was tested.

***Cornus florida* 'Pluribracteata',** a singularly beautiful free-growing, free-flowering form, has six to eight or more broad, slightly twisted floral bracts and true flowers that produce little if any fruit. Flowers emerge about a week after those of most other cultivars (as is the case for most of the "doubles"). Young plants flower

Cornus florida 'Plena'

Cornus florida 'Pluribracteata'

Cornus florida 'Plena'

Cornus florida 'Pluribracteata'

Cornus florida 'Poinsett' (above, below, and below right)

well. Trees are typically open and quite sculptural. They rarely show any spot anthracnose. A particularly memorable specimen grows at the Scott Arboretum of Swarthmore College, Pennsylvania. On one warm summer afternoon, Paul debated the nomenclature of this specimen with Pennsylvania plantsman Bill Barnes. Last Paul heard, Bill was still there trying to convince passersby. This dogwood originated in the early 1900s from Orange County, North Carolina.

Cornus florida **'Poinsett',** a fine selection of Pete Girard of Girard's Nursery in Geneva, Ohio, is a broad-spreading, slow-growing tree with beautiful yellow fruit. The fruit develops a slight red cheek on the sun side not unlike a Golden Delicious apple. The deep red fall foliage around the yellow fruit was the inspiration for the cultivar name. This dogwood is a heavy flowerer and one of the finest forms in the Bernheim Arboretum collection, Clermont, Kentucky.

Cornus florida **'Prairie Pink'** produces apple-blossom pink flowers sparsely on a cold-hardy tree. It supposedly has tolerated −17°F (−27°C) in one evaluation study. This cultivar originated from seed collected by John Pair, Kansas State University, from a population growing in Laramie, Kansas.

Cornus florida **'Prairie Snow'** was selected by John Pair, Kansas State University. Initial budwood was sent to Don for propagation and evaluation, but did not get very far in the process. This cultivar is apparently no longer available.

Cornus florida **'President Ford'** (synonym 'G. H. Ford') is a very vigorous-growing form with variegated foliage of green and yellow, not quite as bright or wide spreading as 'First Lady', and less upright than 'Rainbow'. The leaves remain in good condition throughout the season and finish the show with mottled red and yellow fall foliage. 'President Ford' was introduced by Verkade's Nursery in New Jersey.

Cornus florida var. *pringlei*

Cornus florida **'Presidential'** is listed as a white form with a high susceptibility to powdery mildew.

Cornus florida **var. *pringlei*** is an odd form both horticulturally and botanically. This Mexican taxon produces bracts that remain fused at the tip. Paul has seen this trait demonstrated in two other trees—one in the woods of southern New York State and another in north central Kentucky—but is not sure how these three are or are not related. The bracts make a display reminiscent of a paper lantern.

Cornus florida **'Prosser Red',** one of the earliest of the named red forms, was discovered in 1917 by Bruce Howell, Knoxville, Tennessee, about 3 miles (4.8 km) from his nursery, on land owned by Brown Prosser. Bracts are small but with nice pink color. New foliage also has a reddish tint. This slow grower is also slow to bloom as a young plant. It is likely the same as 'Wine Red' listed by Howell Nursery, Sweetwater, Tennessee, in its 1938 and 1939 catalogs.

Cornus florida **'Pumpkin Patch',** a seedling selection introduced by Don for brilliant orange fall foliage color, also has orange young stems in winter. The plant has shown some mildew susceptibility.

Cornus florida **'Purple Glory'** has deep pink, narrow, and somewhat twisted bracts. Foliage emerges with a purple cast, a hint of which remains through the summer. This dogwood is reasonably resistant to spot anthracnose and is fairly susceptible to stem canker. The selection came from a 1965 seed crop of either an unnamed *C. florida* var. *rubra* or a *C. florida* 'Sweetwater Red' growing at Boyd Nursery of McMinnville, Tennessee. Plant patent number PP4,627.

Cornus florida **'Pygmy'** is an outstanding little plant discovered in a seedling batch by Leon Hawkersmith at Riverside Nursery, Tennessee. The name was inspired by a *National Geographic* article that Hawkersmith was reading at the time of the plant's discovery. He originally thought the true value of this selection would be as a dwarfing interstem on which to graft pink-bracted forms, a use that did not materialize to any significant degree. As the story goes, Hawkersmith showed the original discovery to a group of nurserymen one day and, some time later, the plant mysteriously disappeared out of the nursery row. Fortunately, he had budded a few and so the selection was saved. 'Pygmy' is reasonably resistant to powdery mildew. It is amazing that this fine variety is not in commerce in a large way. Small, compact, and slow growing but always full of floral buds, it eventually makes a dense tree to about 7 feet (2.1 m) tall and 10 feet (3 m) wide.

Cornus florida **'Pygmaea'** is another taxonomic compost pile. A number of forms out there are compact, slow growing, or whatever horticultural euphemism

Cornus florida 'Pumpkin Patch'

Cornus florida 'Pygmy' (above and below)

Cornus florida 'Purple Glory' (above and below)

you care to assign here. Some of them are grand little plants for the landscape. Others should have stayed on the pile from whence they came. There is considerable room for naming here. If there ever was a true 'Pygmaea' out there, it now resides with the passenger pigeon. Straight 'Pygmy' is the way to go here.

Cornus florida **'Rainbow'** produces leaves with a green center and with a white to yellow margin that sometimes show a bit of pink along the extreme edge (possibly only when stressed). The plant has nice red fall color but usually shows a fair amount of spotting by that time of year. 'Rainbow' was discovered as a stump sprout by A. Mazzilli of Canton, Ohio.

Cornus florida **'Red Cloud',** originally tagged 'Webb's Red Cloud', is a pink form with somewhat sparsely set displays of broad, medium pink bracts on a medium-sized tree. Leaf margins are somewhat undulating. The tree shows little fall foliage color. This cultivar was selected and introduced by Webb of Huntsville, Alabama.

Cornus florida **'Red Giant'** bears good-sized flowers but they are far from chasing Jack down the beanstalk. Not sure where the "giant" in the name comes from. Pink bracts are lightest at the tip. This form was selected by Akiri Shibamichi of Japan.

Cornus florida **Red Pygmy**® ('D-383-22') is without a doubt one of the most exciting cultivars of *C. florida* to come along in a long time. This genetic dwarf is ex-

Cornus florida 'Rainbow'   *Cornus florida* 'Red Cloud'

Cornus florida 'Rainbow'

Cornus florida 'Red Cloud'

Cornus florida Red Pygmy®

tremely floriferous as a young plant. A plant 3.5 feet (105 cm) tall may produce as many as 50 blooms. This compact, slow grower with deep pink, somewhat twisted bracts was selected and introduced by Elwin Orton of Rutgers University. Orton had a single plant for several years when one spring, to his horror, he discovered that borers had killed the tree. Fortunately, he had sent several bud sticks to Don a few years earlier, who now had several surviving plants at his nursery.

***Cornus florida* 'Reddy'** reportedly has pink bracts and reddish new growth.

***Cornus florida* 'Redleaf'** also is reported to have pink bracts and red new leaf color. Foliage color supposedly remains better through the summer.

***Cornus florida* 'Rich-red',** presumably a pink-bracted form, is without description.

***Cornus florida* 'Robert's Pink',** a Louisiana selection, offers a vigorous growing pink form for the southern United States. It has shown some susceptibility to spot anthracnose and powdery mildew.

***Cornus florida* 'Rose Valley'** is a light pink form.

***Cornus florida* 'Royal Red',** see 'Cherokee Chief'.

Cornus florida* var. *rubra is generically known as the pink form of the species originally described by Marc Catesby in 1731. Depending on the seed source, one can count on as few as one per 5000 seedlings having pink flowers, or as many as 50 percent. For those who have never grown plants from seed, this variety is a fun one to play with. Seeds of a cultivar such as 'Cherokee Chief' yield a delightful array of bract and foliage color forms. In general, *C. florida* var. *rubra* is purported to be less vigorous and cold tolerant than the species; however, this has never

Cornus florida Red Pygmy®

Cornus florida var. *rubra* (above and below)

Cornus florida 'Rutman'

been put to a test of sufficient rigor. Paul agrees that anecdotally the variety is not as hardy as the species, but he must also have a little Missouri blood in his veins.

***Cornus florida* 'Rutman'** (Wonderberry®; D-184-11) is best described by the trademark name, which says it all. In some years, plants of this cultivar produce large, cylindrical fruit of a brilliant glossy red. Plants show excellent vigor and in early growth have outgrown specimens of 'Sweetwater Red', 'Springtime', and 'Cherokee Princess'. The white bracts have a distinctive red tip. This selection was made by Elwin Orton from a controlled cross of a white seedling and a *C. florida* var. *rubra* seedling. Plant patent number PP8,213.

***Cornus florida* 'Rutnam'** (Red Beauty®; D-376-15) goes by several names. D-376-15 is the name under which it is listed in the U.S. Patent and Trademark office, 'Rutnam' is the name used in trade literature, and Red Beauty® is the name under which it is marketed. By any name, it is a fine plant from the long line of such offerings by Elwin Orton of Rutgers University. It originated as a seedling selection from controlled crosses involving *C. florida* var. *rubra* and *C. florida* 'Pygmy'. The selection is described as being smaller and more compact than 'Cherokee Chief', 'Prosser Red', 'Sweetwater Red', 'Spring Song', and 'Welch's Jr. Miss'; however, it is not a dwarf plant. Bracts are among the deepest reds offered, and the tree is very floriferous. Plant patent number PP8,214.

***Cornus florida* 'Salicifolia'** is a small dense mounded form with very fine texture by virtue of its narrow, straplike leaves. Wyman (1967) credited Maryland nurseryman Henry Hohman with changing his mind about this selection: "Henry J. Hohman of Kingsville Nurseries thinks highly of this variety and has proved to me that uncomplimentary statements I have made about it in the past should be corrected." Do gentlemen like this exist anymore? Flowering is a bit on the light side. This form has been sold under several names, likely including 'Boyd's Willowleaf'.

***Cornus florida* 'September Dog'**. Talk about being in need of some marketing! Unfortunately, in this case, the name is not that far off. This botanical oddity has flower buds that form in late summer and then promptly open. It is certainly better for the flowers in that they don't have to suffer the insults of winter. Since, however, the flowers develop no viable seed, this plant would not be on Darwin's top-ten list. It isn't on Paul's either since the display is fairly spotty.

Cornus florida **'Shadow's Littleleaf'** was selected by Don for tiny leaves, 1 inch (2.5 cm) long and 0.4 inch (9 mm) wide. Bract displays top out at a whopping 2 inches (5 cm) across. Although this plant is not big and bold, it makes a nice little addition to the garden.

Cornus florida **'Shadow's Plena'** was given to Don by Dwight Cain of Spartanburg Landscape Nursery in South Carolina. Large, clean double bracts number up to eight or so on a graceful plant.

Cornus florida 'Shadow's Littleleaf' (above and below)

Cornus florida 'Shadow's Plena'

Cornus florida **'Snow Princess'** is only listed in a powdery mildew rating table under the heading "very susceptible." Presumably it is a white form.

Cornus florida **'Spring Grove',** a seedling selection by Tom Smith from Spring Grove Cemetery in Cincinnati, Ohio, produces enormous masses of white in spring, with bract displays 4–5 inches (10–12.5 cm) across and sometimes produced two or three per stem. This heavy fruiting form also produces excellent rich red fall foliage color. 'Spring Grove' has survived temperatures as low as –26°F (–32°C). It was patented in 1993. Plant patent number PP8,500.

Cornus florida **'Spring Song',** from New Canaan, Connecticut, was selected for its deep pink bracts.

Cornus florida **'Springtime'** has broadly rounded overlapping bracts of clear white on strongly horizontal branches. It is among the earliest cultivars to flower. Leaves show a unique purple tinge on the under sides. The plant shows good mildew and spot anthracnose resistance. This cultivar was selected in 1957 from Spring Grove Cemetery, Cincinnati, Ohio, by E. C. Kern of Wyoming, Ohio. Along with 'Hillenmeyer' and 'Cherokee Princess', 'Springtime' is among the first selected white forms to be grown commercially.

Cornus florida **'Steele's Fastigiate'** is a somewhat upright branching form with large bract displays and excellent quality foliage.

Cornus florida **'Sterling Silver'** was named by Don for its strong creamy variegation that does not burn in full sun. The plant has shown considerable susceptibility to powdery mildew in some areas. It was selected at the Broadview Nursery in Tennessee.

Cornus florida **'Stoke's Pink',** a Louisiana selection, seems to be a good choice for southern gardens by virtue of its low chill requirement. An upright plant, it bears clear pink bracts. Occasionally it is hit fairly heavily by powdery mildew.

Cornus florida **'Sunset'** (Cherokee Sunset™), a wonderful variegated sport of 'Cherokee Chief', shows golden yellow margins and a red stripe at the tip of each leaf. It is vigorous for a variegated form. It has good deep pink bracts. Paul grew 'Sunset' as a foliage plant in his Bangor, Maine, garden for several years; it never flowered as the buds were winter damaged, but the foliage effect was stunning.

Cornus florida 'Sterling Silver' (above and above right)

Cornus florida 'Sunset' (below and below right)

This cultivar shows good spot anthracnose resistance and is a super grower for a variegated form. It was introduced by Commercial Nursery Company, Decherd, Tennessee. Plant patent number PP6,305.

***Cornus florida* 'Sunset Aurea'** has deep pink bracts and moderate yellow leaves.

***Cornus florida* 'Super Dogwood'** is about as bold, vigorous, and robust as the species can get. This selection forms a strong, straight trunk and grows about 50 percent faster than typical for the species. At 18 years of age, the original plant was

Cornus florida 'Super Dogwood' (above and above right)

Cornus florida 'Sweetwater Red'

approximately 28 feet (8.4 m) tall and 22 feet (6.6 m) wide and had a trunk diameter of 12 inches (30 cm). Bracts emerge an ivory color with a slight tinge of pink at the margin. They fade to clear white as they open. 'Super Dogwood' was discovered by Theodore Klein, Crestwood, Kentucky, who also gave us such wonderful garden plants as *Cercis canadensis* 'Silver Cloud', *Cercidiphyllum japonicum* 'Amazing Grace', and many others.

***Cornus florida* 'Sweet Charlotte'**, though rarely listed, was included in trials at Kansas State University. This white form has scarcely been seen since.

***Cornus florida* 'Sweetwater Red'** is one of the most vigorous-growing pink forms. It produces upright branching, deep red-pink bracts, and bronzy new foliage that turns a rich

Cornus florida 'Sweetwater Red'

purple-red in autumn. It was selected in 1954 by Boyd Nursery, McMinnville, Tennessee, and introduced in 1961.

Cornus florida* subsp. *urbiniana is very likely the same as var. *pringlei* in that it is described as having the distinct characteristic of floral bracts fused at the tip. It is represented in literature as seedlings (seed) collected in Nuevo Leon, Mexico.

***Cornus florida* 'Variegata'** once represented a distinct genotype, but it is doubtful that any genetic purity exists in the plants going by this name. The original plant had green leaves with white, rather regular marginal variegation.

***Cornus florida* 'Weaver's White',** a vigorous grower, bears heavy crops of large white bracts on a plant with bold, excellent quality foliage. It is a good selection for the southern United States. Originating from seed collected in northern Florida, it may be the same as a northern Florida selection from the 1940s sometimes referenced as 'Weaver'.

Cornus florida 'Welchii'

Cornus florida **'Welchii'** is sort of the *Fagus sylvatica* 'Roseo-marginata' of the *Cornus* world, but not quite so much of the "roseo." It has green and white leaves, tinged with pink in the spring and summer, and a beautiful mixture of cream, pink, and purple for autumnal dress. This plant is best suited to the shade garden as full sun tends to scorch the creamy portion of the leaves, and it is best adapted to northern gardens in the United States. 'Welchii' has shown considerable spot anthracnose in some areas and has a tendency to revert to the green form. It is occasionally sold under the name 'Tricolor'.

Cornus florida **'Welch's Bay Beauty',** an Alabama selection, is probably the largest-bracted of the so-called double forms out there today. Individual bract displays are in excess of 5 inches (12.5 cm) in diameter and are quite fragrant. Up to seven pairs of broad, overlapping bracts exhibit excellent staying power. The plant has good deep red fall foliage color and a low chill requirement. It was found in Baldwin County, Alabama, in 1972.

Cornus florida **'Welch's Junior Miss'** (synonym 'Junior Miss') has small bracts of rich pink at the tip, fading to almost white at the base. Crisp, clean, and clear, the sparsely produced bracts remain free from spot anthracnose and yield a beautiful display for an unusually long time. Bracts hold their color fairly well in the Deep South of the United States. This cultivar is one of the last to bloom. It was introduced by Chick Welch of Wilmer, Alabama.

Cornus florida **'White Bouquet'** is a compact, rounded plant with very densely set bract displays of purest white.

Cornus florida **'White Catch'** is similar to 'Cloud 9' with wide, heavy-textured white bracts. It is a vigorous plant.

Cornus florida 'White Cloud' (above and below right; above courtesy Erik Fargo)

Cornus florida **'White Cloud',** a fabulous broadly rounded, white bract form, was selected for heavy flowering as a young plant. It was introduced by Wayside Gardens of Mentor, Ohio, before 1946.

Cornus florida **'White Giant'** is a bit of a misnomer. The bracts are a little larger than typical and the plant . . . well, it looks like a good dogwood! There is some indication that this may be a rename of 'Cherokee Princess'.

Cornus florida f. *xanthocarpa*

Cornus florida **'White Love',** introduced by M. Asako of Japan in 2000, is a white, large-bracted and mildew-resistant form. Supposedly the bracts are larger than those of 'Cloud 9' and 'Cherokee Chief'. Plant patent number PP11,654.

Cornus florida **'Williams Red'** was selected from a southern seed source for deep pink-red bracts.

Cornus florida **'Wills'** has dusty green leaves with some white and yellow, irregular marginal variegation, and a bit of wrinkling to the blade. Leaves are smaller than normal and sometimes emerge with a flush of pink. A weak grower, 'Wills' originated as a branch sport of *C. florida* var. *rubra*. It was discovered by Mel Wills of Fairview, Oregon. Plant patent number PP4,300.

Cornus florida **'World's Fair',** a short, stocky grower, flowers at an early age and has been reported to be one of the more bud-hardy forms. It is similar in effect to 'Cloud 9' but flowers about one week later. The original plant was discovered in a seedling block located on Highway 55 in McMinnville, Tennessee. Boyd Nursery Company of McMinnville named it in honor of the 1982 World Energy Fair held in Knoxville. Plant patent number PP4,869.

Cornus florida **f. *xanthocarpa*** is a name applied to plants with many variations on this theme: yellow fruit, often yellowish stems, and pale foliage. There are some standouts floating around that warrant considerable evaluation effort. The forma has been known since 1919.

Cornus angustata
EVERGREEN CHINESE DOGWOOD

Cornus angustata is an evergreen *C. kousa*! What else does one need to say? Talk about a plantsman's mecca—all the attributes of *C. kousa*, with evergreen leaves to boot! This seems like it would be the greatest thing since elasticized socks! Could it really be this good?

In the early 1980s, Ted Dudley of the U.S. National Arboretum ventured to China as part of a Sino-American plant collecting effort. On that trip, he obtained seed and eventually produced seedlings of a taxon then listed as *Cornus kousa* var. *angustata*. Several years later, J. C. Raulston was growing seedlings of the same description from seed obtained from several Chinese botanical gardens. Most plants of *C. angustata* now growing around the southeastern United States derive from these two sources.

Plants of *Cornus angustata* do form beautiful specimens in the right climate. Growing to at least 25 feet (7.5 m) tall with an equal spread, they show the similar creamy white, pointed bracts of *C. kousa* and the bright red fruit that resemble rounded strawberries 1 inch (2.5 cm) in diameter. A mature plant in heavy flower is a sight to behold. It almost looks like a plant of *Ficus benjamina* with *C. kousa* blossoms glued to the branches.

While the evergreen tendencies of *Cornus angustata* vary, the best specimens will hold their foliage nicely throughout a typical winter in USDA hardiness zone 7b or 8. The leaves will turn a dull purple green but most do hold on for at least a good portion of the winter. Farther north, plants can look a bit bedraggled until all the foliage drops. In zone 6 and during hard winters in zone 7, the leaves look tattered and torn. This dogwood definitely needs some protection from desiccating winter winds and will respond nicely to some shade as well. The true flowers are not completely covered by the winter bracts and thus are subject to the vagaries of desiccating winter winds.

Given adequate moisture and the right site, plants are quite vigorous. Todd Lasseigne (pers. comm.) of the JC Raulston Arboretum reports that *Cornus angustata* 'First Choice' grew from 4 to 20 feet (1.2–6 m) tall in 10 years.

Seed propagation requires three months of cold, moist stratification. Softwood cuttings treated with 3000 to 6000 ppm IBA root up to 90 percent in four to five weeks. Cultivars can be budded onto *Cornus angustata*, *C. kousa*, or *C. florida* rootstock.

Cornus angustata 'Elsbry' (Empress of China™) was selected and introduced by South Carolina plantsman John Elsley for its

Cornus angustata 'Elsbry'

spectacular heavy crops of bright white bracts over a long period of time. A plant in full flower will appear almost entirely white. Elsley discovered this selection in 1993 as a young seedling. It flowers in two or three years from grafting and produces its display two weeks later and over a longer period of time as compared to the species. The selection has withstood 0°F (−18°C) without stem or bud damage. It has been fairly free of powdery mildew and shows beautiful glossy dark green leaves that hold their green color better than most cultivars of *C. angustata*. This plant is semi-evergreen in USDA hardiness zones 7–9. It has been budded onto *C. kousa* and *C. florida* understock. Softwood cuttings reportedly root at approximately 80 percent or better. A plant patent has been applied for.

Cornus angustata **'First Choice'** was selected by J. C. Raulston out of the original batch of seed he received from a Chinese botanical garden in the 1980s. The selection was based on the excellent green color of the winter foliage, rootability of cuttings, and superior cold hardiness compared to other seedlings in the planting.

Cornus angustata **'Ticrn'** (Prodigy™) was introduced by Tree Introductions, Athens, Georgia, for improved winter foliage color, uniform growth, and heavy flowering.

Cornus capitata
HIMALAYAN EVERGREEN DOGWOOD, BENTHAM'S CORNEL

A meaningful discussion of why we always want what we can't have is well beyond the scope of this book, but oh what an example we have here. One might think that with all the fabulous plants described in this tome, gardeners might be satisfied. Alas, plantfolk are an insatiable lot, and nowhere in this book would it be more evident than in the case of *Cornus capitata*.

For those who can supply the exacting conditions, this uncommon species forms a fabulously attractive large shrub to small tree up to 40 feet (12 m) tall and wide with broadly arching branches. The leaves are 3–5 inches (7.5–12.5 cm) long and approximately half that in width, extremely glossy, and evergreen. In the United States, this plant is seen best in the Pacific Northwest where specimens grow 10–20 feet (3–6 m) tall, and the foliage remains on the plant through most of the winter. In the southeastern United States, the plant suffers from heat in the summer and cold in the winter.

The June-to-July flowers are not as large as those of *Cornus florida* or *C. kousa* but *en masse* make a fantastic display. Four creamy white to pale yellow, obovate bracts enlarge to 1.5–2 inches (4–5 cm) long, overlap at the base, and tend to point skyward forming a cup. They are held well above the foliage, so put on quite a show with the dark green foil below. The fruits that follow are 1–1.5 inches (2.5–4 cm) in diameter, raspberry-like, and bright red. Most gardeners in the United States will likely see this as one of the parents of several *C. kousa* × *C. capitata* hybrid offerings (for example, 'Norman Hadden' and 'Porlock'). The species is native to western China and the Himalaya.

***Cornus capitata* 'Mountain Moon'** was selected and introduced by Akiri Shibamichi of Japan and brought to North America via Piroche Plants of British Columbia, Canada. It does not seem to exhibit any significant distinguishing characteristics.

***Cornus capitata* subsp. *emeiensis*,** Mt. Emei evergreen dogwood. The taxonomy of the evergreen *Cornus* has been the subject of much confusion and continues to swirl in a "who's on first,

Cornus capitata subsp. *emeiensis* (below and right)

what's on second" in horticultural and botanical literature. This taxon has been variously listed as *C. emeinsis*, *C. omiensis*, *C. omeiensis*, and likely several others. Despite the confusion, it holds considerable hope for those in North America outside the Pacific Northwest with a driving passion for growing something in the *C. capitata* clan. Being generally a more cold hardy form of the species, it will show greater adaptability to the more continental climate on this side of the globe. In several evaluation plantings, plants labeled as 'Summer Passion' have survived temperatures as low as 0°F (–18°C).

***Cornus capitata* subsp. *emeiensis* 'Summer Passion',** a selection from Piroche Plants, Pitt Meadows, British Columbia, represents *C. capitata* subsp. *emeiensis* in the United States. Plants so labeled seem to be rather shy growers that are slow growing and form rather densely branched small trees. Several specimens grown in a Kentucky nursery along with dozens of *C. kousa* cultivars typically showed about one-third the growth of the *C. kousa* cultivars. Some variation may be present as 'Summer Passion' may actually represent a seed strain rather than a clone.

Cornus kousa
CHINESE DOGWOOD, KOUSA DOGWOOD, STRAWBERRY TREE, *YANG-MEI* (CHINESE)

Cornus kousa is the Asian counterpart of the North American native *C. florida*, and it takes center stage as the garden saunters into the warmth of early summer. While it doesn't have the early spring pop of *C. florida*, *C. kousa* shines after most of the garden is dressed in green. And while the species is quite variable with respect to flower timing and fruit show, in general, the show continues from the earliest flowers all the way through summer and into fall. Kousa dogwood definitely fits the cliché of the four-season plant.

In youth, kousa dogwood is upright with a tight vase-shaped habit, generally branched low to the ground. At this stage, it can almost be considered shrublike. With age, it tends to spread along with its tending gardeners, eventually becoming broad and rounded. Mature plants can reach 25–30 feet (7.5–9 m) tall or more with an equal spread. Branches tend to arch out from the base of the tree and unfold to make a fabulous presentation of flowers and fruit.

Leaves of *Cornus kousa* are narrow, ovate to elliptic, up to 4 inches (10 cm) long and a little less than half as wide; they are, deep, often glossy green above (occasionally with blue tones) with lighter green and soft tufts of hairs below. Many of the pink-bracted forms tend to show significant red pigmentation in the major veins and petioles. Fall foliage color is variable, from little or no color to brilliant reds, oranges, and purples. Leaves can occasionally be affected by powdery mildew, which is not nearly as prevalent as it is on *C. florida*.

As with all the large-bracted dogwoods, the true flowers are small and insignificant, borne in umbels 0.5–0.75 inch (12–20 mm) in diameter. Petals are primarily green to brown.

As in *Cornus florida*, the show in *C. kousa* comes from the four bracts of bright to creamy white, or occasionally pink. The white bracts of some forms can develop pink as they age. Those that emerge pink tend to show the color far better in cool climates than in warm. Bracts range from 1 to 3 inches (2.5–7.5 cm) long, some quite narrow and others broad and overlapping. The flowers emerge after the leaves, forming a wonderful contrast. Some selections hold the flowers quite elegantly, high above the leaves for a stunning effect. Flowers last significantly longer than those of *C. florida*.

Cornus kousa

In *Cornus kousa* fruit, the small drupes of red to reddish orange, even pink in some cases, are fused into a raspberry-like fruit (syncarp) up to 1 inch (2.5 cm) in diameter. The flesh is bright yellow to yellow-orange and can be quite sweet. Most are as mealy as an old Red Delicious apple, but the rare tree can produce fruit that is juicy and quite good. Ernest Wilson (1913) described the fruit as "juicy and fair of flavor." Paul once sampled a handful of Prophet™ fruit with John Wachter, and to the surprise of both of them, it was quite good. The fruit hang gracefully on long peduncles up to 2 inches (5 cm) long and may last from several weeks to almost two months.

Once the flowers, foliage, and fruit have left the building, it is time for the bark to have its due. On young plants with branches up to about 2 inches (5 cm) in diameter, bark is smooth and of a uniform gray. Older branches and trunks develop a wonderful exfoliation with shades of gray, copper, and sometimes olive. The presentation is subtle and tends to disappear from a distance, but up close, it makes an excellent winter feature. Large old trees can be quite spectacular.

Like most plants we like to grow in our gardens, *Cornus kousa* loves moist, acidic, well-drained soil with lots of organic matter. If we could just depend on such soil, life in the gardening world would be such a joy. Fortunately, *C. kousa* can handle some

Cornus kousa (below and below right)

Cornus kousa, with sparse flowers

Cornus kousa (the same tree as above), demonstrating the alternate-year
flowering that some trees exhibit.

Cornus kousa (above, below, and below right)

root-zone adversity and still make an excellent show in the garden. While dry, droughty soil is pushing the limit, the species generally takes reasonably well to somewhat heavy soils. Avoid soggy, waterlogged sites and the plant should be fine. Partial shade usually produces fine growth and is downright required for some of the variegated forms, but the best specimens and certainly the best and heaviest flowering comes from plants in full sun.

Cornus kousa is cold hardy to USDA zone 5, although it has potential for solid zone 4 with some new introductions likely to come onto the market over the coming years. In 1984, a U.S. expedition including Paul Meyer of the Morris Arboretum, Darryl Apps, Peter Bristol of the Holden Arboretum, and several others collected seed in South Korea. This Korean collection has yielded plants with excellent cold

hardiness. John Wachter, who was working with Paul at Bernheim Arboretum, Clermont, Kentucky, at the time, tested several accessions in their lab and found more than one plant able to withstand −30°F (−34°C) or better. Stay tuned.

A final general note on *Cornus kousa* concerns the pink-bracted forms on the market today. One only has to access the tip of the information iceberg on the subject to be struck by all the confusion surrounding cultivar characteristics. Some of the early pink introductions came into the United States from Japan. *Cornus kousa* 'Beni Fuji' and 'Miss Satomi' were among the first available to gardeners on this side of the Pacific. Unfortunately, we now find ourselves in the position of having to sort through a whole host of characters, some unique, others renames of existing selections, and still others representing honest labeling mistakes. Recent DNA work done at the University of Tennessee indicated several pink forms sold under different names (Heart Throb™, 'Miss Satomi', and 'Rosabella') to be identical. The easy knee-jerk reaction would be to assume that all originated as renames of the earliest of the group introduced. While this may very well be the case, we must also be open to the possibility that the material brought in for that and other studies simply represents the complete and utter confusion in the trade. In other words, the plants might have been labeled as different forms but may actually represent mislabeled specimens of the same cultivar. The bottom line is that we have an identity crisis in the trade, something that has been with the world of horticulture for a lot longer than pink kousa dogwoods. It is likely to be around long after we are all mulch.

Still, the above situation might have another solution. While there certainly seems to have been some nomenclatural hanky-panky going on with some of the newer introductions, the whole story may be a bit more complicated than meets the eye. A subset of the pink-bracted forms seems to show a set of consistent and alarmingly similar characteristics. *Cornus kousa* Heart Throb™, 'Miss Satomi', and 'Rosabella', along with some seedlings of those named plants, tend to show the same broadly rounded, dark glossy green leaves with distinct red in the major veins. The plants show excellent vigor, generally good fall color, and pink bracts. Gary Handy's Radiant Rose™ also shows these foliage characteristics but seems to perform differently in the field. Other plants could fit this description as well. Could *part* of the answer be that there is a seed strain, or more correctly put, a botanical variety that yields a consistent phenotype? Maybe time will tell, or maybe not.

Seed propagation of *Cornus kousa* requires three months of cold, moist treatment and generally yields high percentage success. Softwood cuttings can be rooted at high IBA concentrations (8,000–12,000 ppm). Most cultivars are grafted or budded with the latter being preferred by most growers.

Cornus kousa 'Akabana'

Cornus kousa 'All Summer' (above and below)

Cornus kousa **'Aget'**, a strong-flowering form, produces additional flowers intermittently through the summer. Bracts are narrow and finely tapered at the apex. Floral bracts can last on the plant for a very long time. The long, narrow leaves are of deep lustrous green. 'Aget' originated as a chance seedling.

Cornus kousa **'Akabana'** is a pink form that may or may not be the same as 'Miss Satomi', 'New Red', 'Rosabella', and possibly a few others. In Japan, the name refers to red or pink shades. This selection is occasionally listed a variegated form, but this is not the case. Todd Lasseigne (pers. comm.) of the JC Raulston Arboretum suggested that this misidentification may represent confusion with 'Akatsuki', which is variegated.

Cornus kousa **'Akatsuki'** was originally found in Japan by Akiri Shibamichi as a sport on 'Miss Satomi'. This selection has green leaves with white edges flushed with pink tones. Bracts are small and mostly white with some pink spotting. As with all the pinks, 'Akatsuki' likely has better color in cooler summer climates.

Cornus kousa **'All Summer'** shows an extended flowering time, often having the latest bracts still on the plant when the first fruit begin to ripen.

Cornus kousa **'Amber'**, introduced by Gary Handy of Handy Nursery Company in Boring, Oregon, has yellow and cream variegation on otherwise green leaves. It is a shrubby grower.

Cornus kousa **'Angela Palmer'** is a variegated form with a bold white-edge variegation on smallish leaves. Plant vigor is a bit reduced compared to the species, and shade seems to be the best home for this fine lady as full sun can burn the foliage.

***Cornus kousa* 'Angyo Dwarf',** a selection of Akiri Shibamichi, was brought into the United States by Barry Yinger and Carl Hahn. Some reports indicate it may not be as small as the name implies, although it may need to be grown on its own roots to show the diminutive character.

***Cornus kousa* 'Autumn Rose'** was introduced by Handy Nursery, Boring, Oregon, after being discovered by the owner's sister, Glenda Schmoyer. Smallish floral bracts fade from pale green to white. Foliage starts the season a light yellow-green and proceeds through a wavy light green

Cornus kousa 'Angela Palmer'

Cornus kousa 'Autumn Rose' (below and below right)

Cornus kousa 'Angyo Dwarf'

summer stage before a spectacular autumn show of pink and red. This semi-dwarf grower has somewhat upright branching.

Cornus kousa 'Avalanche' was selected by Theodore Klein of Yew Dell Gardens, Crestwood, Kentucky. A seedling standout that reportedly survived −30°F (−34°C) during the winter of 1994. The cultivar can be spectacular in flower: broadly rounded, overlapping bracts can cover the entire tree in good years. In light years, the display is a bit spotty. As a young plant, 'Avalanche' takes quite a few years to flower.

Cornus kousa 'Baby Splash' was selected by Gary Handy of Handy Nursery, Boring, Oregon, for white leaf variegation and diminutive leaf and plant size.

Cornus kousa 'Avalanche' (below and below right)

Cornus kousa 'Beni Fuji'

Cornus kousa **'Baier'**, a shrubby, weeping form with dark green leaves and smallish white bracts, comes from Baier Lustgarten, Lustgarten Nurseries in Middle Island, New York.

Cornus kousa **'Beni Fuji'** has among the deepest red bracts of any form on the market today. Like all the pink forms, this one shows best color in cooler summer climates. Bracts are small, narrowly pointed, and produced in large masses most years. Foliage is dark green, glossy and has reddish midribs and petioles. The plant tends to be a shrubby grower. The original seedling came from seed collected in 1970 on the southeastern slopes of Mt. Fuji at an altitude between about 2625 to 3280 feet (800–1000 m) above sea level. It was selected by Nobuo Yamashita, Hisao Ishikawa, and Toshihiro Hagiwara. Plant patent number PP8,676.

Cornus kousa **'Big Apple'** was selected by New England gardener Polly Hill for dark green leathery leaves, large floral bract display up to 5.5 inches (14 cm) in diameter, and huge fruit that approach 1.5 inches (4 cm) in diameter.

Cornus kousa **'Blue Shadow'**, also selected by Polly Hill, was named for Don. It produces deep green-blue foliage with a substantial sheen. This form is one of the very best on the market for foliage quality. Bracts are typical in size and shape but tend to last a long time through the summer. This large-growing and precocious-flowering form can reach more than 30 feet (9 m) in height. It shows excellent heat tolerance.

Cornus kousa 'Big Apple'

Cornus kousa 'Blue Shadow' (above and below)

Cornus kousa **'Bodnant'** features nice displays of broad, rounded, slightly overlapping white bracts and deep green foliage. The winter stems develop a fair purple cast. This form is free-flowering and free-growing.

Cornus kousa **'Bonfire'** was selected for foliage of deep green, light green, and creamy white. Fall color is varied through shades of pink, red, and burgundy. The name may be a bit of overkill, but you get the point. This tree is best if given a bit of shade in the afternoon.

Cornus kousa **'Bultinck's Beauty'** has broad overlapping white bracts and deep green glossy leaves. This selection is often listed incorrectly as "Boltink's Beauty."

Cornus kousa **'Bush's Pink'** was selected as a seedling by Richard Bush of Canby, Oregon. Again, in the Pacific Northwest, the small to medium-sized pink bracts are quite clear and effective. The bract color fades considerably in warmer summers. New foliage has a bit of red that is excellent in the Pacific Northwest, but all but disappears by midsummer farther east.

Cornus kousa **'Camden'** was selected by Mark Stavish of Eastern Plant Specialties in Georgetown, Maine, for its long flowering time and heavy flower crops. In the collection at Bernheim Arboretum, Clermont, Kentucky, the cultivar has flow-

Cornus kousa 'Bonfire'

Cornus kousa 'Camden'

ered sparsely and the flowers that were set did not last noticeably longer than those of the species.

***Cornus kousa* 'Cascade'** has strongly arching branches and medium-wide creamy white bracts on a rounded, smallish plant.

***Cornus kousa* 'Cedar Ridge Select'** was selected by M. Wingle, Cedar Ridge Nursery, Quakertown, Pennsylvania, for its white bracts that turn deep pink tinged as they age.

***Cornus kousa* 'Cherokee'** has wide, rippled bracts set off nicely by dark green, wavy and droopy foliage. The plant has an upright habit that stays with the plant, although it does relax a bit in old age.

***Cornus kousa* 'China Girl',** a Dutch selection made around 1910, is very vigorous and flowers at a very early age. Somewhat sparse in youth, plants fill in as they age. The large floral bracts almost look out of place on young plants. They begin

Cornus kousa 'Cherokee'

Cornus kousa 'China Girl'

small and green and gradually enlarge and brighten to creamy white over time. Rather than developing some pink as they age, these turn brown and drop. Fruit are large, though not as large as those of 'Big Apple'. 'China Girl' is likely a selection of *C. kousa* var. *chinensis*.

Cornus kousa var. chinensis is a nomenclatural conundrum first collected and introduced to the United States by Ernest H. Wilson in 1907. Having studied thoroughly the literature AND the plants (something many of us modern plantsmen, gardeners, students, botanists, taxonomists, and so forth forget to do all too often), Paul believes this taxon represents a superior form of the species. The features do follow successive seed generations and as such the group seems to warrant the variety status.

Wilson described the variety as having fruit that is sweeter than the species. Of course, this is a fellow that one might imagine ingested lead shot rather than Tums® to aid his digestion. Dirr (1998) writes that he prefers Snickers® bars—a statement that will not be debated here.

Trees grown under the *chinensis* label show excellent vigor, a bit earlier flowering than the species, large, broad bracts, and excellent fall foliage color. Wilson (1913) indicated that "this Chinese form will probably prove a better plant under cultivation than the Japanese form with which gardeners are familiar." He definitely hit the nail on the head. Many of the better, more vigorous cultivars on the market are selections of var. *chinensis*.

Cornus kousa var. *chinensis*

Now, not to diverge too indiscreetly here, but later in the same writing, Wilson waxed eloquent about his collecting in northwest Hubei province in China. He described the horrible weather as "with a healthy dose of thick mist thrown in for good measure," adding, "but the display of the day was made by the wild roses . . . *Rosa multiflora*—both white and pink forms." Oh, how times have changed. Had Wilson tried to bring back his newfound prizes today, he would have been flogged as an importer of the unclean, the wretched, and the cruel. Amazing how one generation's prize is another's curse. Oh, if I had a nickel for every . . .

***Cornus kousa* 'Chiprizam'** (Christian Prince™) is a name from Lake County Nursery of Ohio and attributed to plants that bear white bracts on a small to medium-sized tree.

***Cornus kousa* 'Claudia',** a selection of var. *chinensis,* has not been widely distributed. A plant growing at the Royal Horticultural Society Garden at Wisley was received in 1999 from nurseryman Mark Bulk of the Netherlands.

***Cornus kousa* 'Crème Puff',** a broad-spreading selection that develops into a shrubby plant, offers heavy flowering and excellent deep brick red fall foliage. This cultivar was selected by master plant propagator Bill Barnes of Lorax Farms, Warrington, Pennsylvania.

***Cornus kousa* 'Doubloon'** was selected by William Devine, Kennedyville, Maryland, in the early 1970s for upright growth habit and semi-double bract displays. It is a sister seedling of *C. kousa* 'Parasol'.

Cornus kousa 'Crème Puff'. Photo courtesy Bill Barnes

Cornus kousa **'Dr. Bump'**, a densely branched, shrubby selection, is heavy flowering and can develop excellent exfoliating bark.

Cornus kousa **'Dwarf Pink'** was introduced to the United States by Barry Yinger of Hines Nursery and Carl Hahn of Brookside Gardens, Wheaton, Maryland, for slender pink bracts produced on a compact, upright grower. Bract color is somewhat unpredictable, ranging from deep red to almost white depending on the year. This dogwood can be grown on its own roots. Indeed, it should be so grown to keep its compact habit. The original plant was found by Akiri Shibamichi in Gumma Prefecture, Japan.

Cornus kousa **'Ed Mezitt'**, a name with great genes (jeans), honors a great plantsman and nurseryman who introduced many wonderful plants to our gardens. What would New England gardens be without the PJM group of rhododendrons and all PJ's sister siblings? Having lived through 10 Maine winters, Paul can attest that spring would have been a far more somber event. Fortunately for the younger generation, Ed's son Wayne continues the heritage of great plants. But we digress . . . again. The cultivar in question was selected from a batch of open-pollinated seedlings of a *C. kousa* × *C. kousa* var. *chinensis* parent, for purple new growth and bright orange-red fall foliage color. It has wide, overlapping bracts.

Cornus kousa **'Elizabeth Lustgarten'** is best described as a stiff weeper. Not the graceful bends of *Salix alba* 'Tristis' or others of the kind, this tree has pendulous

Cornus kousa 'Dr. Bump'

Cornus kousa 'Dwarf Pink'

tendencies most appropriately classified as moderate. It will make a medium-sized tree up to about 10 feet (3 m) tall and 5 feet (1.5 m) wide in 10 to 12 years. Of all the weepers on the market, this one has the largest and broadest bracts. White bracts tend to age through a bit of pink. They overlap at the base unlike those of 'Weaver's Weeping' that tend to stay separate from tip to base. The original seedling was selected by Jim Cross, of Environmentals in New York, from seedlings produced by Baier Lustgarten, Lustgarten Nurseries in Middle Island, New York.

***Cornus kousa* 'Elmwood Weeper'** is a weeping selection very similar, if not identical, to 'Weaver's Weeping'.

***Cornus kousa* 'Emerald Star'** has deep green foliage with mid-sized displays of rounded white bracts that seldom overlap.

***Cornus kousa* 'Endurance'** was selected and introduced by Weston Nurseries, Hopkinton, Massachusetts, for floral bracts with great staying power. Could the name have been inspired by the famed Boston Marathon which used to begin right outside the nursery's front door?

***Cornus kousa* 'Fanfare'** was selected by Polly Wakefield of Milton, Massachusetts, for strong upright growth and hardiness to −20°F (−29°C). Plant patent number PP3,296.

Cornus kousa 'Elizabeth Lustgarten'

Cornus kousa 'Emerald Star'

***Cornus kousa* 'Fireworks',** a selection of *C. kousa* var. *chinensis*, has brilliant fall foliage of yellow, red, and a little purple.

Cornus kousa 'Galzam'

Cornus kousa **'Flowertime'** is a heavy-flowering form with wide bracts. It flowers at an early age but can have occasional light-flowering years.

Cornus kousa **'Galzam'** (Galilean®), one of the Biblical Series™ from Lake County Nursery, Ohio, is a form of *C. kousa* var. *chinensis*. It produces large, bold bract displays. Bracts are wide-rounded at the base and narrowly pointed at the tip. Leaves are deep, glossy green, broadly rounded with deeply impressed veins. 'Galzam' is an excellent foliage form. Plants will grow 20–25 feet (6–7.5 m) tall by 15–20 feet (4.5–6 m) wide. They are reportedly a bit more cold tolerant than typical for the species.

Cornus kousa **'Gay Head'** is an unusual selection by Polly Hill for upright growth and narrow pointed, somewhat rumpled bracts.

Cornus kousa **'Girard's Nana'**, a nice dwarf form growing 6 inches (15 cm) or less per year and producing a surprisingly good floral display, was selected by Girard's Nursery of Ohio.

Cornus kousa **'Gold Cup'**, a vigorous-growing selection from New Zealand, has dark green margins and a bright yellow blotch in the center. It is among the better yellow-centered leaf forms. Bracts are white. Foliage quality is better and growth stronger and more upright than that of 'Gold Star'. 'Gold Cup' holds its leaf color very well throughout the season.

Cornus kousa **'Gold Star'** is an excellent if somewhat slow-growing form with a strong gold center to each leaf that holds up well through the season. Amazingly, the foliage remains in excellent condition through late summer even sited in full Kentucky sun. In such a site, the leaves will cup a bit, but the color and overall foliage quality hang in there nicely. In shade, the plant is much more open, but still a striking specimen. 'Gold Star' was selected and introduced by the Sakata Nursery in Yokohama, Japan, and listed in their spring 1978 catalog. It was introduced to the United States by Barry Yinger of Hines Nursery, Irvine, California, and Carl Hahn of Brookside Gardens, Wheaton, Maryland.

Cornus kousa 'Gay Head'

Cornus kousa 'Girard's Nana' (above and below)

Cornus kousa 'Gold Star'

Cornus kousa 'Greensleeves'

***Cornus kousa* 'Greensleeves'** was selected by Polly Wakefield of Milton, Massachusetts, for outstanding large, deep green, very glossy leaves with a wavy margin, and floral bracts that retain a fair amount of green pigmentation. The deep emerald leaf color, bold texture, and excellent gloss help this cultivar stand out in the crowd. It has excellent vigor, keeping pace with some of the typically more vigorous *C. kousa* × *C. florida* hybrids. The bracts are quite large and broad, overlapping the basal half of each, and held nicely above the foliage for an excellent display. Oddly enough, plants growing in the shade tend to lose their green bract pigmentation far sooner than those in full sun. Similar to 'Moonbeam'. Overall, 'Greensleeves' is one of the very best *C. kousa* cultivars available. It is likely a selection of var. *chinensis*.

***Cornus kousa* 'Greta's Gold'** is a bold form with bronzy new leaves that mature to medium green with a bright gold marginal splash. This selection of *C. kousa* var. *chinensis* originated as a branch sport in the nursery of PMA Plant Specialties and was named by the Junkers for their baby daughter Greta. The variegation was apparently unstable initially. Fall foliage color is a wonderful mix of pink and red following the variegation pattern.

***Cornus kousa* 'Grumpy'**, a very small grower with narrow, creased leaves and limited flowering, may have originated at the Handy Nursery, Boring, Oregon.

***Cornus kousa* 'Hanros'** (Radiant Rose™) was selected by Gary Handy of Handy Nursery, Boring, Oregon, from a seedling batch of pink-bracted seedlings. Compared to 'Miss Satomi', 'Hanros' shows deeper green foliage, dark red-maroon fall color, and in the Pacific Northwest better red bract color. Handy (pers. comm.) also reports this selection to retain better quality foliage in the summer. In the eastern United States, the color is good but not as rich as in the Northwest. Fall color is excellent deep red. The fruit is large and quite rounded, looking more like

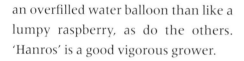
Cornus kousa 'Hanros'

Cornus kousa 'Highland' (above and below)

an overfilled water balloon than like a lumpy raspberry, as do the others. 'Hanros' is a good vigorous grower.

***Cornus kousa* 'Highland'** is a cold-hardy selection from Highland Park in Rochester, New York. Plants flower heavily and at a rather young age. Bracts are more of an ivory hue than clear white. This slow grower produces light green foliage on a broad plant.

***Cornus kousa* 'John Slocock'** may not be a commonly found selection, but two plants can be found growing at the Royal Horticultural Society Garden at Rosemoor, Devon. The plants have very dark green, glossy leaves with bright yellow veins. The creamy white floral bracts have broadly rounded tips and age through a slightly

blotched pink stage. The Rosemoor plants were received in 2001 from Spinner's Nursery in Lymington, Hampshire, United Kingdom.

Cornus kousa **'Julian',** a Poly Hill introduction named for her husband, this selection was made for clear white bracts, up-curved at the tip, excellent fall color, and rather large fruit.

Cornus kousa **'July Jubilee'** is a dark green leaf form with fairly good bract display that tends to last quite late into the summer.

Cornus kousa **'Kalmthout'**, a selection of *C. kousa* var. *chinensis*, has excellent vigor and broad, bold floral bracts. Two specimens grow at the Royal Horticultural Society Garden at Wisley. Plants were received from nurseryman Mark Bulk in Boskoop, Netherlands. This dogwood was not introduced by the Belgian arboretum of the same name.

Cornus kousa **'Kirkpatrick's Weeping'** will make somewhat of a tree on its own after only a bit of initial staking. It is more upright growing than other weepers, although a little on the slow side.

Cornus kousa **'Kordes',** a heavy-blooming form with broadly rounded bracts, is an inconsistent bloomer but not necessarily alternate-year blooming. When it shines, however, few can rival its display. This dogwood was selected by Kordes Jungpflanzen, Bilsen, Germany.

Cornus kousa **'Kreuzdame'** is listed without description.

Cornus kousa **'Kristin Lipka's Variegated Weeper',** a sport of either 'Lustgarten Weeping' or 'Elizabeth Lustgarten', has stiff weeping tendencies and creamy margins to otherwise dark green leaves. It has reasonable vigor for a variegated form but tends to throw reversions from time to time and leaves can burn a bit in the summer if planted in full sun. Flowers are subtended by moderate-sized bracts that open creamy in the center with a greenish margin, fading to all creamy white over time. Fall foliage color is a mix of purple, yellow, and green following the summer variegation pattern. This dogwood was selected by Robert Lipka of Cedar Farm, Cedars, Pennsylvania, and named for his daughter. Plant patent number PP13,384.

Cornus kousa **'Laura'** is listed only as a white-bracted form.

Cornus kousa **'Little Beauty',** selected by J. C. Raulston out of a batch of seedlings from South Korea, has white bracts and subtly variegated leaves. The plant grows about 6 inches (15 cm) per year, eventually forming a squat, broad-spreading specimen.

Cornus kousa **'Little China',** a diminutive selection introduced by Mr. Gilardelli of Milan, Italy, is one of the few extreme dwarfs that flowers heavily.

Cornus kousa **'Luce',** an invalid name, is described as cold hardy to –30°F (–34°C). It is reported to have been named in honor of Roger Luce, Butternut Hill Farm, Newburgh, Maine. While Luce certainly deserves such an honor, the story is only partially correct. The tree exists as described; however, it has not been named or formally introduced as it is still under evaluation.

Cornus kousa **'Lustgarten Weeping',** a Jim Cross selection from the same batch of seedlings as 'Elizabeth Lustgarten', is certainly a distinct plant. If not staked, the

Cornus kousa 'Lustgarten Weeping'

Cornus kousa 'Madame Butterfly

plant will creep, weep, and wind its way to a 2- to 3-foot (60- to 90-cm) tall groundcover. It is an outstanding form for draping over a wall. Flowers and bracts are held nicely above the foliage. Imagine using this as an espalier along a brick wall or chimney. The effect would be spectacular.

***Cornus kousa* 'Madame Butterfly'** is a name with two forms. Could this be a true case of parallel evolution? One form is a vigorous grower with heavy crops of narrow pointed floral bracts that point skyward at the tip. This form was selected by David Leach of North Madison, Ohio. The second form came to the U.S. National Arboretum via Peter Chappell in England. It is an exceptionally large-bracted form with individual displays in excess of 5 inches (12.5 cm) in diameter.

***Cornus kousa* 'Madison'** (Crown Jewel™) begins the season with typical *C. kousa* foliage and flower characteristics; however, later in the summer, the new growth emerges a brilliant yellow-gold with red hints. The effect is quite spectacular but is only produced when the tree flushes new growth in the heat of the summer. Plants that do not put on the second flush of growth never show the bright coloration. In the Pacific Northwest where summer temperatures are lower than elsewhere, the color is not as pronounced. 'Madison' was selected and introduced by Tim Brotzman of Brotzman's Nursery, Madison, Ohio.

***Cornus kousa* 'Marble',** a Cedar Ridge Farms introduction, has swirled creamy variegation to the leaves. It was selected and named by Robert Lipka of Cedars, Pennsylvania.

***Cornus kousa* 'Milky Way'** was originally described as a selection of *C. kousa* var. *chinensis* with the typically robust growth, heavy flowering and fruiting, and large floral bracts of the variety. All sounds good, doesn't it? Talk about a confused mess! One can find catalog listings of this dogwood under the names "True Milky Way," "Milky Way Seedlings," "Milky Way Select Seedlings," "Certified Correct Milky Way," and even "Milky Way—propagated from THE original plant!" Unlike other confused, horticultural messes, this one has a history that is traceable. It is not likely correctable though. Dirr (1990) provided an excellent synopsis of the history based on conversations with Elwin Orton of Rutgers University.

In the 1960s, Wayside Gardens had a field of several thousand seedlings of *Cornus kousa*, which were grown from seed obtained from many different plants. The seedlings in this field were evaluated for floral characteristics, with primary emphasis on larger floral bracts and precocious flowering. About 15 plants that Mr. Silvieus said were truly outstanding in these characteristics were selected and transplanted to the corner of a field at the 100-acre [40-hectare] production nursery Wayside Gardens maintained at Perry, Ohio. These selected plants constituted the "stock block" from which scionwood was taken for use in propagating plants of 'Milky Way' by budding.

Thus, an "original" 'Milky Way' plant traces to any one of approximately 15 different seedlings resulting from seed collected from many open-pollinated plants. Present-day "seedlings of 'Milky Way'" would thus be open-pollinated seedling propagules of any one of those approximately 15 original open-pollinated (self-sterile) seedlings, and one would expect them to be highly variable.

Cornus kousa 'Milky Way'

***Cornus kousa* 'Milky Way Select',** a selected seedling of 'Milky Way', shows the characteristics of the "original" and has been asexually propagated. Plants are very vigorous and heavy flowering with broad overlapping bracts. This form was introduced by Deb McCowan of Knight Hollow Nursery, Middleton, Wisconsin.

Cornus kousa 'Milky Way Select'

***Cornus kousa* 'Minuma',** a semi-double selection, bears up to six bracts on most of the blooms on the tree. It was selected by Toshihiro Hagiwara of Japan.

***Cornus kousa* 'Miss Petty'** has leaves that are slightly cupped and almost black-green, among the darkest of the *C. kousa* selections. Clean white bracts overlap through the basal half and age through a bit of pink.

***Cornus kousa* 'Miss Satomi'** (synonym 'Satomi') is one of the first of the pink-bracted forms introduced to the United States. Leaves are deep glossy green, wide, and rounded with deeply impressed veins that show some red coloration. DNA research at the University of Tennessee indicates this to be the same form as 'Rosabella' and 'Heart Throb™, but distinct from Samaritan™ and Christian Prince™. At least the three pinks so labeled and tested turned out to be the same. They are so confused, who knows what was actually tested, and this point was raised in the original report. 'Miss Satomi', as it is represented in the market material today, is still probably one of the best of the pink forms; it actually has pink pigmentation at times other than severe drought stress—some other supposedly pink-bracted forms can be kept white as long as the irrigation system doesn't clog. 'Miss Satomi'

Cornus kousa 'Miss Satomi'

Cornus kousa 'Rosabella'

was selected and introduced by Akiri Shibamichi of Japan. A columnar sport of 'Miss Satomi' has been discovered by Mr. Gilardelli of Milan, Italy.

Cornus kousa 'Moonbeam'

Cornus kousa 'Moonbeam' is described as having floral bract displays 7–8 inches (17.5–20 cm) in diameter, set nicely above deep, glossy green foliage. It is also reported to be cold hardy to −20°F (−29°C). Polly Wakefield of Milton, Massachusetts, introduced this selection. Bracts are broad, overlap along the lower half, and tend to droop at the tips. Displays of 7 to 8 inches in diameter would only be the description offered by one who dabbles in trout fishing! The excellent deep green leaves are similar to those of 'Greensleeves'. 'Moonbeam' is a very vigorous but somewhat open grower.

Cornus kousa **'Moonlight'**, also introduced by Polly Wakefield, is similar to 'Moonbeam' with less floppy bracts.

Cornus kousa **'Moonsplash'**, a Gary Handy (Boring, Oregon) selection under evaluation, is described by Gary as being similar to 'Sunsplash'.

Cornus kousa **'National'** is a large, very vigorous, vase-shaped tree producing large, ivory-white broad, overlapping bracts set flat above the foliage. The large fruit are up to 1.5 inches (4 cm) in diameter.

Cornus kousa **'Nell Monk'**, a heavy-flowering form with wide, overlapping bracts, is a seedling selection originating at Nyman's Garden in Sussex, England, in 1968.

Cornus kousa **'New Red'** is very likely the same as 'Miss Satomi'.

Cornus kousa **'Nicole'** was selected by Mr. Gilardelli of Milan, Italy, and named for his daughter.

Cornus kousa **'Par Four'** was selected for heavily set displays of wide, overlapping bracts.

Cornus kousa **'Parasol'** has large, bright white overlapping bracts with rounded tips, on a strongly arching tree. Each bloom has to up eight or more bracts. The tree displays excellent red fall foliage color. The selection originated from open-pollinated seed of an unnamed *C. kousa* plant growing in Silver Spring, Montgomery County, Maryland. A sister seedling to 'Doubloon', 'Parasol' was selected by William Devine of Kennedyville, Maryland. Plant patent number PP8,703.

Cornus kousa **'Pendula'** is a shrubby, strongly pendulous, and very densely branched form with fairly reliable flowering. It tends to flower more heavily than the pendulous *C. florida* selections. Eventually it reaches 10 feet (3 m) tall and 8 feet (2.4 m) wide.

Cornus kousa **'Peve Limbo'** is without description.

Cornus kousa **'Pollywood'**, a large, robust-growing tree with large, sharp-pointed, late-opening and long-lasting bracts, was selected by Polly Hill.

Cornus kousa 'National'

Cornus kousa 'Nicole'

Cornus kousa 'Pendula'

Cornus kousa 'Pollywood'

Cornus kousa 'Propzam'

***Cornus kousa* 'Propzam'** (Prophet™), one of the Biblical Series™ from Lake County Nursery, Ohio, was selected from a *C. kousa* var. *chinesis* seedlot. Plants develop large, slightly overlapping floral bracts in continuous sprays along each branch. Blooms tend to be a bit smaller than those of Galilean®. Foliage has a thick and substantial texture of rich green in summer and a deep red-maroon in autumn. 'Propzam' is one of the better foliage forms on the market. Large plump fruit are as sweet-tasting as any when ripe.

***Cornus kousa* 'Prolific',** a 1968 selection from Grootendorst and Sons, Boskoop, Holland, has somewhat early opening flowers with bracts of clean white.

***Cornus kousa* 'Rasen'** bears broad, creamy white, heavily overlapping bracts that become heavily reflexed at maturity.

***Cornus kousa* Raulston Selection,** a seedling from South Korea collected by J. C. Raulston, has exhibited evergreen tendencies. It is not officially registered or named as of this writing.

***Cornus kousa* 'Repeat'** tends to have a second, albeit reduced bloom in late summer. It was introduced by Richard Bush of Canby, Oregon.

***Cornus kousa* 'Repeat Bloomer'** was selected by J. G. Marano Jr. of Doylestown, Pennsylvania, for large white bracts produced over a protracted period.

***Cornus kousa* 'Rochester'**, a large vigorous selection made by Hoogendorn Nursery of Newport, Rhode Island, has exceptionally large bracts.

Cornus kousa 'Rochester'

Cornus kousa 'Rochester' (above and above right)

***Cornus kousa* 'Rosea'** may have been a valid cultivar name at some point in history, but those days are likely gone. Like so many 'Rosea' pseudotaxa in the plant world, this has become a bit of a taxonomic compost pile. Most likely, the best way to treat this bit is as var. *rosea*. An exceptionally wonderful plant under this name grows at the Royal Horticultural Society Garden at Rosemoor, Devon. According to Karan Junker (pers. comm.) of PMA Plant Specialties, many British gardeners lust after this plant. Seems everyone wants the Rosemoor plant. Karan's suggestion is to name the particular plant 'Rosemoor Pink' to set it apart from the others. Sounds like a good idea.

***Cornus kousa* 'Rubra'** is listed by several references as an introduction of Henry J. Hohman, Kingsville, Maryland, but the plant does not seem to be in the trade.

***Cornus kousa* 'S. Hoffen'** is a small, shrubby form that is a touch on the slow-growing side. Leaves are gray-green in the center, surrounded by a chalky white. Compared to 'Wolf Eyes', 'S. Hoffen' is not as vigorous and its leaves crease along the midrib more and have wavier margins. Bracts are narrowly pointed and small; the entire bloom typically measuring not more than 2.5 inches (6.5 cm) across. 'S. Hoffen' is definitely a plant for shady situations.

Cornus kousa 'S. Hoffen'

Cornus kousa 'Samzam' (above and below)

Cornus kousa 'Samzam' (Samaritan®), one of the Biblical Series™ from Lake County Nursery, Ohio, is a seedling of 'Milky Way' selected for its creamy white edge variegation on leaves with a slightly undulating margin. Nice creamy white bracts that tend to get lost in the foliage. Leaves stay in good condition all summer long. Fall foliage is pink and maroon.

Cornus kousa 'Schmetterling' is an upright grower with large white bracts. It was introduced by Firma C. Esveld, Boskoop, Netherlands.

Cornus kousa 'Schmred' (Heart Throb™) was named and introduced by Jim Schmidt of Don Schmidt Nursery, Boring, Oregon, for large deep pink floral bracts on a large, broad-spreading tree. Leaves are glossy green with red at the tip. DNA research at the University of Tennessee has

Cornus kousa 'Schmred'

Cornus kousa 'Silver Cup'

indicated this to be the same as 'Miss Satomi' and 'Rosabella'. The plants Paul has seen look identical, but the material circulating around the industry is likely completely confused. Plant patent number PP9,283.

***Cornus kousa* 'Select',** a product of Select Trees in Athens, Georgia, looks almost like 'Greensleeves' without the green in the bracts. Leaves are large, deep glossy green but lack the undulation of 'Greensleeves'.

***Cornus kousa* 'Silver Cup'** was selected by Polly Wakefield of Milton, Massachusetts, for upturned bracts that almost form a cuplike display.

***Cornus kousa* 'Silver Phesant'** was selected by Mark Bulk of Boskoop, Netherlands, for white variegation over deep green. It is a vigorous grower but may not be entirely stable.

***Cornus kousa* 'Silver Splash',** selected by Gary Handy of Handy Nursery, Boring, Oregon, who described it as producing "awesome twisted green, white, and pink variegation on new growth but as is the case with most plants with this type of foliage it disappears after the plant gains maturity." This dogwood is no longer in production.

***Cornus kousa* 'Silverstar'** is a vigorous, upright vase-shaped grower cold hardy to –20°F (–29°C). It has the typical flower and bract display. This form was selected by Polly Wakefield, Milton, Massachusetts, in 1972. Plant patent number PP3,261.

***Cornus kousa* 'Simpson #1'** is a heavy-flowering, broad-spreading form that can reach more than 20 feet (6 m) wide over time. It comes from the Simpson Nursery of Vincennes, Indiana.

Cornus kousa 'Simpson #1'

Cornus kousa 'Simpson #2'

***Cornus kousa* 'Simpson #2'** is very similar to 'Simpson #1' in vigor, foliage, and flower production. This selection is significantly more upright, growing to 25 feet (7.5 m) tall by 18 feet (5.4 m) wide. It also is from the Simpson Nursery of Vincennes, Indiana.

***Cornus kousa* 'Snowbird',** a small, slow-growing, compact grower with small leaves and bracts, was selected by Polly Hill of Massachusetts.

***Cornus kousa* 'Snowboy'** has soft white-edged gray-green leaves that are less harsh than some of the new variegated upstarts. It is definitely a plant for

Cornus kousa 'Snowboy' (above and below)

those with high shade and a patient hand. In the United States, the plant tends to revert and is severely limited in the vigor category. Yet across the pond, Karen Junker (pers. comm.) of Junker's Nursery "won the prestigious Award of Merit with this spectacular plant at Les Journées des Plants de Courson." 'Snowboy' was selected and introduced into cultivation by the Sakata Nursery of Yokahama, Japan, and introduced to the United States by Barry Yinger of Hines Nursery, Irvine, California, and Carl Hahn of Brookside Gardens, Wheaton, Maryland.

***Cornus kousa* 'Snow Flake'** is listed as a selection of *C. kousa* var. *chinensis* with all the typical accolades of heavy flowering, non-overlapping medium to large, somewhat wavy bracts, and large fruit. It is not seen often.

***Cornus kousa* 'Southern Cross'** is a stocky, somewhat shrubby form from New Zealand with abundant, creamy

Cornus kousa 'Snow Flake'

white bracts that mature through a distinct pink phase. It has excellent red fall foliage.

***Cornus kousa* 'Speciosa'** is a form with wavy dark green margins and large, broad clear white overlapping bracts. The plant is slow growing. 'Speciosa' was selected and introduced by the Dutch nursery of J. Blaauw and Company in 1952.

***Cornus kousa* 'Spinners',** supposedly of the var. *chinensis* lineage, is heavy flowering and fruiting with fruit held nicely above the foliage. It has long, narrow pointed bracts. This selection is a robust grower.

***Cornus kousa* 'Square Dance',** another in the long procession of introductions from Polly Hill, Martha's Vineyard, Massachusetts, was named by Pamela Harper for the four overlapping, large bracts in a somewhat "go to your corner" arrangement. Fruits are large and held just above the foliage.

***Cornus kousa* 'Steeple'** was selected by Polly Hill for distinct upright growth habit, good fall foliage color, and excellent deep green, glossy foliage. Bracts are sharp pointed at the tip.

***Cornus kousa* 'Summer Games'** is a weak grower but seems to be stable. Paul was first shown this plant by Wayne Mezitt of Weston Nurseries, Hopkinton, Massachusetts. Wayne selected this plant for its splashed cream and green foliage.

***Cornus kousa* 'Summer Majesty'** was selected by Mitsch Nursery of Aurora, Oregon, and named by Diane Fincham for heavily produced white bracts that

Cornus kousa 'Square Dance'

Cornus kousa 'Steeple'

Cornus kousa 'Steeple'

Cornus kousa 'Summer Stars'

mature through a distinct pink stage. Flowers last for up to eight weeks in the Pacific Northwest, possibly five or so weeks in the Midwest. Growth is somewhat wispy and open, but the overall effect is quite nice.

***Cornus kousa* 'Summer Stars'** has floral bracts that hold on for a long time and some are actually present when fruits begin to color. This upright oval form has good fall foliage color. It was discovered as a chance seedling in the late 1960s by Peter Costitch of Center Moriches, Long Island, New York. Plant patent number PP3,090.

***Cornus kousa* 'Sunsplash',** a bright green palette edged with brilliant yellow on spring leaves, is slow-growing and shrubby. The leaves do not burn in the sun in

Cornus kousa 'Sunsplash'

Cornus kousa 'Temple Jewel' (above and below)

the Pacific Northwest. Fall foliage color is a nice mix of reds, yellows, and oranges. 'Sunsplash' was selected by Gary Handy of Handy Nursery, Boring, Oregon.

***Cornus kousa* 'Temple Jewel'** is a 1970s selection from Brotzman's Nursery, Madison, Ohio. The following description comes from well-known and much-respected plantsman and nurseryman Tim Brotzman, who also introduced us to such novelties as *Cercis canadensis* 'Covey' (Lavender Twist®) and others. New foliage on 'Temple Jewel' emerges green with a light yellow irregular central blotch. As the leaves mature, they go almost entirely green, just a tad lighter in the center. Late season flushes of growth will also show the light yellow central blotch. This somewhat densely branched grower bears white bracts that occasionally show a rim of pale green.

The selection originated in a batch of seedlings purchased from nurseryman Paul Otto of Perry, Ohio. Otto had collected the seed from a group of several large trees selected out of the *Cornus kousa* var. *chinensis* 'Milky Way' seed strain. The original plant produced the sport described here and also had a green-white variegated sport that, according to Tim Brotzman (pers. comm.), resembled *C. kousa* 'Wolf Eyes' but was obviously distinct as it arose spontaneously at his nursery. While Brotzman reports an occasional green reversion in his 'Temple Jewel' production block, he has never witnessed another sport of green-white variegation from plants of 'Temple Jewel'.

***Cornus kousa* 'Teutonia'** is occasionally listed but without description.

***Cornus kousa* 'Ticknor's Choice'** is an odd selection for bract color, which begins green, fades to white, and instead of aging through cream or pink, seems to go back to its green roots. This form was selected by Robert Ticknor, North Willamette Research and Extension Center, Aurora, Oregon.

***Cornus kousa* 'Trinity Star'** was selected by Gary Handy of Handy Nursery, Boring, Oregon, for heavy foliage of green, white, and pink, an effect that fades

Cornus kousa 'Ticknor's Choice'

Cornus kousa 'Trinity Star'

Cornus kousa 'Ticknor's Choice'

Cornus kousa 'Trinity Star'

through the summer. The plant produces excellent crops of clean white bracts. Handy (pers. comm.) describes this small, compact grower as semi-dwarf.

***Cornus kousa* 'Triple Crown'** was patented by Polly Wakefield of Milton, Massachusetts, for fine-textured growth, broad, dark green, somewhat pendulous leaves, and heavy clustered flowering. The plant tends to produce small bouquets of "flowers" at the ends of some of the branches. This good, cold-hardy selection has flowered after experiencing −20°F (−29°C). Plant patent number PP3,387.

***Cornus kousa* 'Tsukuba No Mine'** is a shy, shrubby grower with thin branches and a densely twiggy habit. Bracts are creamy white, small, narrow, and pointed, with no overlap. The plant was selected and introduced by Nobuo Yamashita, Hisao Ishikawa, and Toshihiro Hagiwara from a batch of *C. kousa* seed collected near Numata city in Gumma Prefecture, Japan, in October 1978. Plant patent number PP8,518

***Cornus kousa* 'Twinkle'** is a Polly Wakefield introduction that produces flowers subtended by six to nine bracts and excellent deep red fall foliage color. The plant habit is upright. Plant patent number PP3,386.

***Cornus kousa* 'Variegata'** is another of the taxonomic bowls of pasta. One form under this name has leaves of gray-green, white, and a little stress-induced pink. It seems to be a rather stable if not a very pretty form, lacking supremely in vigor. A plant in Elwin Orton's collection at Rutgers University shows much more striking variegation on some branches but alas is highly unstable. The Arnold Arboretum has a form that shows greater vigor than the previous two mentioned here. As far as this cultivar name goes, buyer beware!

***Cornus kousa* 'Victory'** is another of the cup-forming forms with bracts turned upward at the tip. It is heavy flowering and vigorous growing. 'Victory' was selected by Jon Arnow of Fairfield, Connecticut.

Cornus kousa 'Variegata'

***Cornus kousa* 'Viridis'** is listed in one reference only—at the Arnold Arboretum. The source listed was A. Coffin, Locust Valley, New York.

***Cornus kousa* 'Waterfall'** is among the most pendulous of the weepers. This green leaf form will simply creep along the ground if it is not staked.

***Cornus kousa* 'Weaver's Weeping'**, probably one of the strongest weepers, is a heavy flowering form with the flowers set nicely above the foliage. Bracts are long, pointed, and narrow; they are primarily white but do run through a brief pink stage as they fade. May be the same as 'Elmwood Weeper'.

Cornus kousa 'Variegata'

Cornus kousa 'Weaver's Weeping'

Cornus kousa **'Weberiana'** is listed without description.

Cornus kousa **'Weisse Fontane',** a selection of Firma C. Esveld, Boskoop, Netherlands, is a weeping form that tends to be a bit more stiffly branched than 'Weaver's Weeping'.

Cornus kousa **'Whirlwind',** a rather odd selection, develops spirally swept branches in early growth. It makes one want to look for Dorothy and Toto amid the branches. The plant does grow out of this habit with time.

Cornus kousa **'White Dream'** is listed without description.

Cornus kousa **'White Dusted'** has bright green leaves. The bracts are narrowly pointed, yielding a fine, dainty display.

Cornus kousa **'White Fountain'** is a broad-growing form with wide, arching branches. Heavily produced masses of bracts emerge about two weeks later than most *C. kousa* selections.

Cornus kousa **'Wieting'** (synonym 'Wieting's Select') is a vigorous selection made for brilliant red and orange fall foliage color. All other characteristics are typical of *C. kousa* var. *chinensis* selections.

Cornus kousa **'Willamette',** a 1995 Oregon introduction, yields vigorous growth, dark green foliage, and heavy flowering. Are we sounding like a broken record yet?

Cornus kousa **'Wilton'** was originally introduced by Hoogendorn Nursery of Newport, Rhode Island, as 'Wiltoni' but is now sold under 'Wilton'. It has long-lasting creamy white bracts. This plant is rarely encountered today.

Cornus kousa **'Wisley Queen'** is identified as a *C. kousa* var. *chinensis* selection by Jim Gardiner, curator of the Royal Horticultural Society Garden at Wisley.

Cornus kousa **'Wolf Eyes'** is, without doubt, among the best of the white-variegated forms. Originally discovered as a sport at Manor View Farm, Monkton, Maryland, it has a strong white margin that is reliably stable (ok, maybe it reverts occasionally) and holds up well under the searing sun of a Kentucky summer.

Cornus kousa 'Wolf Eyes' (above and above right)

Shrubby in growth, six-year-old plants measure 5 feet (1.5 m) tall and 7 feet (2.1 m) wide. This selection has worked well in heavy shade, providing a delightful bright spot in a dark garden. In such a site the leaves remain flat rather than curling. In full sun the leaves crease along the midrib and develop a wavy margin while retaining their color. Master-grafter Harald Neubauer of Belvidere, Tennessee, grows many dogwoods. While most of his one-year-old *C. kousa* buds reach 5–6 feet (1.5–1.8 m) tall, those of 'Wolf Eyes' typically top out at about 3 feet (90 cm) tall. With all the great introductions out there, this is a true standout.

Cornus kousa 'Xanthocarpa', a yellow-fruited selection, has been described in the European literature since the 1950s. It originated in the Netherlands.

Cornus nuttallii
PACIFIC DOGWOOD

Cornus nuttallii is essentially the western analog of *C. florida*, its range spanning from British Columbia to mid or southern California. The typical specimen grows to be a medium tree to 25 feet (7.5 m) or more in height, more upright and vigorous in growth compared to its eastern cousin. As a garden plant, it is rarely seen outside its native range owing primarily to limited adaptability. Strangely, even through its own backyard, while used in gardens and landscapes, the species and its cultivars have never created quite the fervor of the flowering dogwood in the East.

The floral display of *Cornus nuttallii* is similar to but quite distinct from *C. florida*. In Pacific dogwood, blooms tend to have six showy bracts of creamy white to, just occasionally, a bit of a pink tinge. Blooms with four, five, or even seven or eight bracts can be found but are not as common as those with six. The full bract displays are typically 3.5 inches (9 cm) to as much as 5 inches (12.5 cm) across with the occasional plant showing displays up to 8 inches (20 cm). Bracts are flat to reflexed at maturity and some bear distinct longitudinal ribbing. In winter dress, the bracts do not cover the flowers, leaving the winter flower buds subject to desiccation. Occasionally, some of the bracts may enlarge in the fall, yielding a straggly partial show. Of course, this results in another partial show in the spring. The true flowers are purple to green and lack fragrance.

Leaves of *Cornus nuttallii* are simple, opposite, and ovate, tending to be a bit larger than those of *C. florida*. Summer color is deep green with some specimens showing significant gloss through the season. Fall color can range from wanting to very nice reds and oranges. Fruit is similar to but larger than *C. florida*. Plants of *C. nuttallii* rarely set more than one or two fruits per inflorescence.

Cornus nuttallii is definitely a plant for the cool, moderate climate of the Pacific Northwest. In the East, the plant struggles, and flower buds blast below about 0 to −5°F (−18 to −21°C). Stem survival is dubious below this temperature as well. This

Cornus nuttallii (below and below right)

dogwood is essentially like most people, preferring moderate temperatures, not too cold and not too warm. One of the problems with growing the species in the East is that it often fails to stop growing in time to shut down and harden for the winter.

Pacific dogwood has shown considerable susceptibility to dogwood anthracnose, the first signs of which were discovered in Washington State in 1979. The species also suffers to varying degrees from powdery mildew and spot anthracnose. As with *Cornus florida*, borers are a problem primarily on stressed trees.

Seed propagation requires three to five months of cold stratification. Cuttings root, but resultant plants are of poorer quality than those from budding or seed.

***Cornus nuttallii* 'Barrick'** is a large-bracted, free-flowering form with blooms reaching 5–6 inches (12.5–15 cm) in diameter. Bracts are deeply ridged with a cleft at the tip of each.

***Cornus nuttallii* 'Boyd's Hardy'** is the sole plant to survive in a Tennessee-grown seedling batch following a −19°F (−28°C) winter in 1964.

***Cornus nuttallii* 'Colrigo Giant',** when in the right home, is a robust, large-growing form with large bract displays from 6 to 8 inches (15–20 cm). It is nothing short of drop-to-one's-knees amazing. Leaves are deep green and leathery. One might speculate that this is a polyploid. Paul has grown this cultivar in Ken-

Cornus nuttallii 'Barrick'   *Cornus nuttallii* 'Colrigo Giant'

tucky and has to rate it as miserable. The leaves curl and burn and, although in container culture with ample moisture it does grow quickly, the growth is a bit gawky, almost rank. This cultivar is named for the *Col*umbia *Riv*er *Gor*ge where it was discovered.

***Cornus nuttallii* 'Colrigo Wonder'** is similar to its "giant" cousin but not quite as large or robust.

***Cornus nuttallii* 'Eddiei'** was listed by Wyman (1967, p. 168) as found in the wild in 1918 by H. H. Eddie, a nurseryman of Vancouver, British Columbia. It was described as having leaves spotted and mottled with gold. This cultivar is seldom found listed in other references. Oddly, *C.* 'Eddie's White Wonder' is sometimes incorrectly listed in nursery catalogs as species or variety *eddiei*.

***Cornus nuttallii* 'Goldspot'** has large floppy leaves that look as if the house painters forgot to tarp the tree. In warmer areas, the gold flecks turn a not-so-alluring shopping-bag brown. Pointed floral bracts are large and often show a fair amount of green at the base. This cultivar produces heavy crops of flowers and, as with many selections of the species, may do a bit of a minor floral dance in the fall.

Cornus nuttallii 'Goldspot' (below and below right)

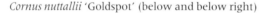

An excellent mixture of deep red and a little orange is displayed in areas where the leaves remain in good condition throughout the season. Krüssman (1984) described the selection as being "without particular garden merit." Ouch!

Cornus nuttallii **'Monarch'** is one of the wider selections of this species with beautifully layered branching. It eventually grows almost twice as wide as tall. Bracts are more rounded than most and the new branches emerge with a distinct purple color. Fall color is vivid red.

Cornus nuttallii **'North Star',** an upright, vigorous grower, produces large bract displays up to 6 inches (15 cm) or more in diameter. Bracts are pointed and barely overlap. New shoot growth is purple and fall foliage is a good deep red color.

Cornus nuttallii **'Pilgrim',** a southern selection found along State Route 17 in or around Santa Cruz County, California, has smaller bract displays than most, 4 inches (10 cm).

Cornus nuttallii **'Portlemouth'** has large, broad, and ridged floral bracts beautifully presented on a somewhat upright tree. Like most, it may show partial flowering in autumn. Fall foliage colors are mostly mixed reds. The plant apparently originated as a chance seedling in a garden near Salcombe, Devon, England.

Cornus florida Group Hybrids

Hybrids have been made using four species in this group: *Cornus capitata, C. florida, C. kousa*, and *C. nuttallii*.

Cornus capitata × C. florida

Cornus **'Floricap'** is a barely known hybrid that has not been tested around much. A young plant at the JC Raulston Arboretum of North Carolina State University has shown reasonable growth with characteristics somewhat halfway between the two parents. It does not seem to be overly vigorous.

Cornus florida × C. nuttallii

Cornus florida × *C. nuttallii* hybrids, in general, show more *C. nuttallii* characteristics than *C. florida*. Winter flower buds remain mostly uncovered by the bracts, stem growth tends toward the more rank growth of *C. nuttallii*, and cold hardiness follows suit. These hybrids are all best grown in the same regions as Pacific dogwood. Temperatures much below 0 to −5°F (−18 to −20°C) result in bud blast and stem die back. Still, in the right climate, some of these selections form singularly beautiful trees.

***Cornus* 'Ascona'** will form a tree 20–25 feet (6–7.5 m) tall with spreading, somewhat pendulous branches that reach for the ground. The white bracts are similar to those of *C. florida* but are deeply ridged and slightly recurved toward the tip. The arching branches clothed in white bracts make a fabulous graceful scene. This cultivar has excellent red fall foliage in areas where the plant performs well.

***Cornus* 'Eddie's White Wonder'** (*C. florida* × *C. nuttallii*) can make quite a statement in the Pacific Northwest landscape. It is vigorous, almost to a fault. At first quite upright, plants later begin to spread, eventually developing somewhat pendulous branches. Bract displays are large, flat, and clear white. Fall foliage color can be an impressive deep red.

Unfortunately, in the East, living plants are none too impressive. Actually, in all but the Northwest, the plant is a floppy, rank grower, prone to flower bud blast, bark split, and a host of other maladies. Not that this is untrue for most of the *Cornus nuttallii* cultivars growing east of the Rockies. It's just that 'Eddie's White Wonder', the result of a marriage of first cousins, was supposed to be the savior for eastern and midwestern growers who wanted a *C. nuttallii* for their palette. In short, however, the offspring got the bigger ears rather than the bigger brain!

Donald Wyman (1967) described a letter from J. H. Eddie of H. M. Eddie and Sons, Vancouver, British Columbia, in which was described a hybrid of *Cornus florida* and *C. nuttallii* made by his father H. M. Eddie. The plant was described as having pendulous branches, leaves like *C. florida* (only larger), and flowers like *C. nuttallii*. The letter described the blossoms as being up to 6 inches (15 cm) across. And thus was born 'Eddie's White Wonder'.

Cornus nuttallii 'Eddie's White Wonder'

In Europe, there seems to be a second form also sold under the same name. Several sources describe a fairly upright form that does not spread with age.

***Cornus* 'Ormonde',** with upward-tending branches, produces a more narrow plant with healthy quantities of large, broad white bracts, occasionally with a pink tinge. Fall color can be a brilliant mix of pinks and reds.

Cornus **'Pink Blush'** (a presumed cross of *C. nuttallii* × *C. florida*) has been billed in some offerings as a pink 'Eddie's White Wonder' which might be good news for some and dreadful billing in other parts of the world. In the right place, plants are vigorous, with wonderfully layered branches on a broad tree. The large bracts are pale pink in color. Introduced by Handy Nursery, Boring, Oregon, 'Pink Blush' originated as seed of *C. nuttallii* growing in a yard where *C. florida* var. *rubra* also grew.

Cornus kousa × C. capitata

Cornus **'Norman Hadden'** is a beautiful tree, 20–30 feet (6–9 m) tall, that originated at Porlock, Somerset, England. The original plant now resides at Knightshayes Court, Devon. Creamy white, tapered floral bracts in June turn deep to pale pink with age. In autumn, the plant forms large strawberry-like fruits typical of *C. capitata*. The bark exfoliates somewhat like *C. kousa* but not to the same extent. It thrives in a sheltered, partially shaded site, seemingly fairly intolerant of heat and cold. It does best is USDA hardiness zone 6b with cool summers. Think Seattle or Portland. In the United Kingdom, the plant requires a fair amount of sun to ripen the late summer stems. There, it is also semi-evergreen, depending on the winter conditions.

Cornus **'Porlock'** originated in the garden of Norman Hadden and forms a smaller plant than 'Norman Hadden'.

Cornus 'Porlock'

Cornus kousa × C. florida

This cross, known as *Cornus* ×*rutgersensis*, is represented by a group of hybrids developed by Elwin Orton of Rutgers University, New Brunswick, New Jersey. In 1961 Orton began a hybridization program to combine the best characteristics of *C. florida* and *C. kousa*. After more than 20 years of work, Orton and Rutgers released a group of six patented cultivars under the trademarked names Aurora®, Constellation®, Celestial®, Ruth Ellen®, Stellar Pink®, and Stardust®. All six exhibit intermediate characteristics with Ruth Ellen® and Stardust® being the closest to the *C. florida* parent. The remaining four more closely favor *C. kousa*.

These hybrids are low branched, mostly with strongly ascending tendencies and an upright overall shape. Flowering time begins with Ruth Ellen® just as the last of the *Cornus florida* fade, with Constellation® being about the latest to flower. Bract display ranges from no overlap in Constellation® to heavy overlap in Aurora®. Bracts of most are a substantial creamy white. Bracts of Ruth Ellen® are a gleaming clear white when fully open. Stellar Pink® can exhibit a pale pink color as the bracts open, while Stardust® and Ruth Ellen® begin white and can fade to a significant pink. Aurora® and Constellation® show the least pink as the bracts age. In favorable springs (cool, with little wind) all the hybrids can flower for a month or more. The plants are sterile, producing only occasional seeds, all hollow or flattened and deformed.

One of the most outstanding features of these hybrids as a group is the tremendous vigor exhibited by young plants. A cultivar screening Paul began with John Wachter in 1998 included more than 100 named cultivars. The hybrids could be spotted immediately in a quick observation of more than 500 container-grown plants: they towered above almost all the others.

The hybrids seem to be free from the powdery mildew that so plagues many *Cornus florida* plants. Borer susceptibility seems to be the same as for both parents; stressed plants are usually short lived. Plants kept free from stress, however, tend to stay free from borers. The hybrids presented here have also shown themselves to be relatively free from dogwood anthracnose. Only scant reports of foliar lesions have shown up in the literature.

***Cornus ×rutgersensis* 'Rutban'** (Aurora®), a distinctly upright grower in youth, becomes broader with age. This hybrid has the best summer foliage of the group:

Cornus ×rutgersensis 'Rutban' (below and below right)

Cornus ×rutgersensis 'Rutban'

Cornus ×rutgersensis 'Rutcan' (above and below)

deep green and thick in texture. Fall foliage is a wonderful deep red with lighter highlights. Bracts are broad and overlapping at the base and of a clear creamy white, taking on some pink toward the end of the flowering season. Aurora® flowers with Celestial®. It is listed in the title of the patent application under the cultivar name 'Aurora' but designated 'Rutban' within the body of the document. Patented in 1990. Plant patent number PP7,205.

***Cornus ×rutgersensis* 'Rutcan'** (Constellation®), an upright grower, is the most vigorous of the group, the original plant being 21 feet (6.3 m) tall and 17 feet (5.1 m) wide at 19 years. It has also remained the most vigorous after 30 years of growth. The floral bracts are distinctly obovate with an acute tip, do not overlap, and are longer than the bracts of Stardust®.

Cornus ×rutgersensis 'Rutdan' (above and below)

Constellation® produces the fewest true flowers per inflorescence (25) of all the original *C. ×rutgersensis* hybrids. Flowers open two to three days after Ruth Ellen® and Stardust®. Very little if any pink develops in the bracts as they age. Constellation® resulted from a cross of an unnamed *C. kousa* and *C. florida* 'Cherokee Princess'. Plant patent number PP7,210 awarded in April of 1990. The patent application approved is under the name Constellation® but then designated as 'Rutcan' in the body of the text.

***Cornus ×rutgersensis* 'Rutdan'** (Celestial®), originally patented under the name 'Galaxy', is an upright grower with white flowers and broadly rounded bracts that almost overlap. They emerge four to five days after Ruth Ellen®. The bracts bend upward at the midpoint to form a bit of a cup but do relax to a flat display with time. This selection is not as vigorous and bracts are not as wide as those of Aurora®. True flowers are also more exposed in winter bud than are those of Aurora®. After 19 years, the original plant measured 17 feet (5.1 m) tall and 14 feet (4.2 m) wide. Celestial® resulted from a cross of unnamed *C. kousa* and unnamed *C. florida*. Plant patent number PP7,204.

***Cornus ×rutgersensis* 'Rutfan'** (Stardust®), also like *C. florida*, is the lowest and widest growing of the group. At 19 years of age, the original plant was 11 feet (3.3 m) tall and 19 feet (5.7 m) wide and very densely branched to the ground. Flowering is a day or two later than Ruth Ellen®. Bracts are broad obovate and do not overlap even at full size. Stardust® has not gotten the spread of the others, primarily due to graft incompatibility problems; however, some growers have had luck rooting softwood cuttings treated with 1000 to 3000 ppm K-IBA. This hybrid was named for the deceased wife of a former president of Rutgers University. Plant patent number PP7,206.

***Cornus ×rutgersensis* 'Rutgan'** (Stellar Pink®) begins somewhat upright, maturing to a rounded plant with age. The original plant measured 20 feet (6 m) tall and 19 feet (5.7 m) wide after 19 years. The bracts are broadly rounded, slightly overlapping, and white to soft pink, depending on the year. Stellar Pink® originated as a hybrid of an unnamed *C. kousa* and *C. florida* 'Sweetwater Red'. Plant patent number PP7,207. The title of

Cornus ×rutgersensis 'Rutfan'

Cornus ×rutgersensis 'Rutgan'

Cornus ×rutgersensis 'Rutgan'

Cornus ×rutgersensis 'Rutlan' (below and right)

the patent application lists Stellar Pink® and then goes on to say that the selection "should be denominated as 'Rutgan'."

***Cornus ×rutgersensis* 'Rutlan'** (Ruth Ellen®) is one of the *C. ×rutgersensis* hybrids that most closely resembles the *C. florida* parent. Specimens are low branched and wide spreading, even at a young age. Floral bracts are intermediate in shape and size as is the case for all the hybrids. Bracts emerge just as the last of the *C. florida* bracts are fading, making Ruth Ellen® the first of the *C. ×rutgersensis* hybrids to flower. The slightly overlapping bracts provide for a brilliant white display for three weeks or more and can take on significant pink tones as

they age. Ruth Ellen® generally has fewer true flowers per inflorescence than Aurora®, Celestial®, and Stellar Pink®. At 19 years of age, the original tree was 18 feet (5.4 m) tall and 22 feet (6.6 m) wide. It resulted from a cross of an un-named *C. kousa* and *C. florida* 'Hillenmeyer'. It was patented in 1991. Plant patent number PP7,732.

Cornus ×rutgersensis Saturn™ was one of the original hybrids made by Orton but was not named with the original six. Don considers this selection to be at least as good as any of the original introductions. It is a very vigorous, rounded grower that most closely resembles Celestial® in growth and form. Bracts are bright white, broad ovate, and overlap significantly. Foliage is a wonderful deep lustrous green. While some of the original *C. ×rutgersensis* hybrids had begun to slow down in growth at more than 30 years of age, the original plant of Saturn® was still show-ing excellent vigor and no branch decline. Plant patent applied for.

Cornus ×rutgersensis Saturn™ (below and below right)

Cornus kousa × *C. nuttallii*

Cornus **'KN30-8'** (Venus™) is a marvelous product of the famed dogwood breeder Elwin Orton of Rutgers University. A cross of *C. kousa* × *C. nuttallii* by an unrelated *C. kousa*, this has the largest bracts of all Orton's hybrids. The bract display is typically 5–6 inches (12.5–15 cm) in diameter, occasionally up to 7 inches (17.5 cm)—and not the mythical 6 inches (15 cm) of some published reports of other cultivars. Bracts are clear white with no pink. The foliage is an excellent deep green color and has substantial constitution. True flowers are mostly enclosed in the winter bracts. At 15 years of age, the original plant measured 18 feet (5.4 m) tall and 25 (7.5 m) feet wide. This plant will become a staple in the landscape industry very quickly. Plant patent to be applied for.

Cornus **'KN4-43'** (Starlight™), another of Orton's hybrids, originates from a cross of *C. kousa* × *C. nuttallii*. It is a strong-growing plant with excellent dark green foliage and four wide, partially overlapping creamy white bracts yielding displays of up to 5 inches (12.5 cm) across. True flowers are not covered by the winter bracts. At 30 years of age, the original plant was 30 feet (9 m) tall and 20 feet (6 m) wide and still quite vigorous. Plant patent to be applied for.

Cornus 'KN30-8'

Cornus 'KN4-43'

Cornus 'KN30-8'

CHAPTER 6

THE
Cornus mas
GROUP

The members of the *Cornus mas* group, while excellent garden plants in their own right, are perceived as suffering from a bit of bract envy in the eyes of the general public. But while they do lack the large showy bracts of some of their compatriots, the early sulfur-yellow, before much else gets going in the late winter garden, is a worthy trait. They are tough and adaptable and suffer few problems in the garden.

Cornus mas
CORNELIAN CHERRY DOGWOOD

Cornus mas is one of the most often overlooked of the dogwood species. As a garden plant, it offers multiseason interest, outstanding adaptability, and tremendous flexibility. Early spring flowers, excellent summer foliage and fruit, and tolerance of both sun and shade—it would seem the cornelian cherry dogwood could find a place in most landscapes.

The species is best described as a large, densely branched shrub or small tree 18–25 feet (5.4–7.5 m) tall, occasionally more, upright in youth but spreading to broad, and arching with age. While it can be limbed up and grown as a small tree, such pruning results in a rather disheveled look. It is far better as a multitrunked specimen where it forms a densely branched mass of fine twiggy stems all the way to the ground.

While there are a number of attributes that should win *Cornus mas* a spot on just about any gardener's palette, it is the flowers that get top billing. Opening in mid to late March in Kentucky, the bright, fresh yellow flowers are borne in umbels, 1 inch (2.5 cm) in diameter, and clothe just about every branch. While individually the flowers are nothing to write home about at 0.25–0.4 inch (6–9 mm) in diameter, their early emergence and the quantity produced make the show worth the price of admission. Indeed, if *C. mas* bloomed in May, we'd hardly notice with all the exuberant display of the less-humble plants in the garden; but to the winter-weary gardener looking for some significant sign of spring, this is an indispensable selection. For those unable to await Mother Nature's seasonal cue, the cut stems force wonderfully for a bright winter bouquet. Through the dormant season, the flowers are enclosed in a lightbulb-shaped bud of four overlapping bracts. The ancients referred to *C. mas* as male cornel since the first flowers to appear on young plants are typically all male.

Come warmer weather, ovate to elliptic leaves up to 4 inches (10 cm) long and 2.5 inches (6.5 cm) wide are typically a bright glossy green all summer long. Leaves show deeply impressed veins and can develop a leathery texture on some plants. Fall foliage color is at best a bit of purple and yellow but is seldom overwhelming.

Cornus mas (below, below right, and opposite)

Cornus mas

Fruit of *Cornus mas* does not have the same show power as some of its glitzier brethren, but the subtle effect is a nice close-up feature. The oblong drupes are up to 0.75 inch (2 cm) long and 0.6 inch (16 mm) wide, occasionally pear shaped. They ripen in mid to late summer to a glossy, scarlet red and rarely yellow. The stone is large, taking up to 80 percent of the volume of the fruit. Being mostly self-sterile like most dogwoods, isolated plants of *C. mas* tend to set poor fruit crops. The ripe pulp varies tremendously in flavor from horrendously astringent to downright delicious. Regardless of the individual plant's culinary characteristics, the fruit don't reach their peak of flavor until about 30 seconds before they drop off the tree. Of course, the birds know that as well and seem to beat the gardener to the punch by a day or two. The birds must speak the same language as sweet-corn-eating raccoons, as both seem to understand three words in the English language: one more day.

Cornus mas fruit makes excellent preserves and jellies. Linda Mitchell, wife of University of Maine landscape architect Bill Mitchell, makes the best *C. mas* jelly anywhere on the planet. It is sweet and tart at the same time. All gardeners should keep a jar of this in their refrigerator to test their gardening friends' powers of plant identification.

When it comes to bark, *Cornus mas* is often described as offering some such nonsense as "delightfully flaky and exfoliating." In reality, the bark is marginally interesting to a plant geek and described by many nonbelievers as just plain brown.

In the culture world, *Cornus mas* moves to the head of the class as one of the easiest of the large dogwoods to grow. It transplants readily and will take just about any soil from dry to wet. At Bernheim Arboretum, Clermont, Kentucky, a thriving if slow-growing specimen of 'Variegata' can be found on a very dry shady hillside. Just 100 yards (91 m) away is a fabulous mass of the species in a low, waterlogged meadow planting. The species and its cultivars adapt to a wide range of pH and soil textures.

Cornus mas is also tolerant of heavy pruning. It can be pruned up unto a nice little three- to five-stemmed small tree (with a considerable amount of work) and can even be sheared into a nice little hedge. An outstanding example of a *C. mas* hedge can be found at the Chicago Botanic Garden.

One 2000 report indicated *Cornus mas* susceptibility to *Pseudomonas syringae*.

The natural range of *Cornus mas* extends from central and southern Europe through western Asia.

Seed propagation of *Cornus mas* takes patience. Seed requires a warm, moist stratification for up to 120 days followed by 90 to 120 days of cold. Softwood cuttings treated with 3000 to 8000 ppm IBA root at reasonably high percentages but take their own sweet time. Cultivars can be budded onto *C. mas* rootstock.

Cornus mas **'Alba'** is reported in the literature as a white-fruited clone.

Cornus mas **'Aurea'** is a bright yellow-green form (more yellow in full sun, more green in shade) with moderate growth. It is somewhat susceptible to leaf spot, especially if drought stressed in the sun. Keep in slight shade and well watered. It is very cold hardy, surviving a −30°F (−34°C) winter at the University of Maine.

Cornus mas **'Crispa'**, as the name implies, has leaves that are a bit shriveled and puckered along the margin. It was obviously named before PR departments were employed to come up with marketable sales names for new plants of questionable merit. This form is a collector's plant at best.

Cornus mas **'Elegant'**, from the Central Botanic Garden in Kiev, was selected for longer-than-normal, bright red fruit.

Cornus mas **'Elegantissima'** is a lovely form with brightly colored leaves variegated pink, yellow, and green. It is fairly susceptible to leaf spot, shy to flower, and best grown in afternoon shade. 'Elegantissima' is sometimes listed as 'Aureo-elegantissima' or 'Tricolor'.

Cornus mas **'Flava'** ('Xanthocarpa', as it is sometimes listed) is, in Paul's opinion, a cultivar rather than a variety since he has grown several seed populations from a so-named plant and never had a yellow-fruited form show up in the batch.

Cornus mas 'Flava'

Cornus mas 'Golden Glory'

The fruits are yellow with a red cheek, and they are reasonably sweet. This good, cold-hardy form survived –30°F (–34°C) with only minor flower bud damage. Some nursery catalogs occasional list 'Yellow' which is very likely the same thing.

***Cornus mas* 'Golden Glory'** has deep green leaves and prolific flowering, especially as a young plant. It is a bit more tender than some, showing considerable damage at –20°F (–29°C) . A specimen died to the ground at –30°F (–34°C) at the University of Maine. 'Golden Glory' was introduced by Synnesvedt Nursery, Glenview, Illinois.

***Cornus mas* 'Grovemas'** is an invalid name once attributed to a variegated form from Spring Grove Cemetery in Cincinnati, Ohio. The plant turned out to be quite unstable and was never registered.

***Cornus mas* 'Helen',** a Russian introduction, was selected for production of large juicy red fruit.

***Cornus mas* 'Hillier's Upright'** is an upright grower with large fruit from the Sir Harold Hillier Gardens and Arboretum.

***Cornus mas* 'Jolico',** a rarely seen selection, is described as heavy flowering with large quantities of deep, rich red, large fruit.

***Cornus mas* 'Lanceolata'** was described by Krüssman (1984) as having narrow, lanceolate leaves edged in white. This selection is likely not in commerce any longer.

***Cornus mas* 'Macrocarpa'** is a large-fruited form with all other characteristics as described for the species.

Cornus mas **'Morris Arboretum'** is another large-fruited selection.

Cornus mas **'Nana',** described as a small form growing up to about 6 feet (1.8 m) tall and 5 feet (1.5 m) wide, is slow growing but otherwise similar to the species. Wyman (1967) described having ordered this cultivar numerous times from European nurseries only to receive *C. pumila* instead. 'Nana' supposedly originated in the mid 1800s.

Cornus mas **'National Arboretum Variegated'** is not actually a registered cultivar; however, it has been bouncing around the United States for some time. Actually it is fairly unstable and sports all kinds of variegated white, yellow, and green shoots. One could name a hundred distinct foliage forms from a single plant. Unfortunately, few, if any, would be stable.

Cornus mas **'Pioneer'** has very large pear-shaped red fruit. This form was introduced from northern Europe.

Cornus mas **'Pyramidalis',** an upright selection described in some older literature, may or may not be in cultivation any longer.

Cornus mas **'Redstone'** is a seed-produced cultivar from the National Plant Materials Center in Ellsberry, Missouri. It was selected for its adaptability, pest resistance (which basically means that it is a *C. mas*!), and heavy fruit production. Fruits are up to 0.6 inch 1.5 cm) long and described as tart but edible. With so many good selections out there, this form is probably not worth the gardener's time. It might be good for naturalizing if a known provenance strain is desired. One of the original plants was 20 feet (6 m) tall and 22–24 feet (6.6–7.3 m) wide after 44 years. Now that's an evaluation!

Cornus mas **f. sphaerocarpa** is distinguished by its round fruit as opposed to the oblong fruit typical of the species.

Cornus mas **'Spring Glow',** a J. C. Raulston introduction, is one of the best for the southern United States. It has a lower chill requirement than others and flowers well in the warmer climes of Dixie. It is limited in the northern United States though in that it has shown significant bud kill at −20°F (−29°C) and died to the ground at −30°F (−34°C) at the University of Maine. Root rot may be a problem in heavy soils.

Cornus mas 'Variegata' (above and below)

***Cornus mas* 'Spring Sun'** (originally named 'Spring Grove') supposedly is a non-suckering form with heavy flower and fruit set and dark, glossy green leaves of a thick constitution.

***Cornus mas* 'Ukraine',** a cold-hardy form tolerant down to −30°F (−34°C), has large, pear-shaped fruit bearing juicy tart flesh. The fruit are a brilliant cherry red. With selections like this available to gardeners, why would anyone deal with the hassle of growing sour cherries?

***Cornus mas* 'Variegata'**—talk about an overlooked plant—has smallish ovate leaves with a uniform, clear white margin and a gray-green center. This form is quite stable. It is best grown in shade to avoid burning the white portions. A slower grower than most and also more shrub than tree, 'Variegata' holds up nicely in the landscape and flowers freely. The plant even seems to perform nicely in rather dry shade once established. It would be nice to see this one in more gardens.

***Cornus mas* 'Vidubetskii'** (Redstar™) bears large, bright cherry red fruit that is oblong and quite tart. Plants produce large crops each year. This form is very cold hardy and vigorous.

***Cornus mas* 'Violacea',** an older selection, bears typical growth, flowers, and foliage. Fruit ripens to a deep purple blue.

Cornus chinensis

Cornus chinensis is best described as a black-fruited, large-leafed, and minimally cold-hardy *C. mas*. Bright yellow March flowers about 50 percent larger than those of *C. mas* give way to ovate-elliptical flat green leaves, typically up to 6 inches (15 cm) long, occasionally to 10 inches (25 cm) long. The leaves have deeply impressed veins and heavy white pubescence beneath. From southern and central China, this species is cold hardy to USDA zones 8–9. It has been cultivated in the West from about the mid-twentieth century.

Cornus officinalis
JAPANESE CORNEL DOGWOOD

Cornus officinalis has garnered much attention of late as various plant award programs look to push the public's plant envelope. And it is not a bad plant to push at all. Think of this as a somewhat smaller, more heavily flowering, generally showier, and more eastern version of *C. mas*. While some describe the flowers as being a brighter yellow than *C. mas*, any difference is overshadowed by seedling variation in both species. *Cornus officinalis* tends to flower a week or two earlier than its western cousin and this may give it a leg up in the eyes of some. The heavy masses of sulfur yellow can open as early as the first week of March in Kentucky and seem to be slightly more frost tolerant than are those of *C. mas*. The fruit are similar in set, size, and color, but some describe them as being far less palatable. The primary difference in fruit between the two species is that while *C. mas* fruit ripen in July or August, those of *C. officinalis* are not fully ripe until at least mid-September. As a garden plant, *C. officinalis* tends to be smaller, with a stiffer and more open branching. It is probably a better plant for the small to medium garden than is *C. mas*.

Cornus officinalis

From an ID standpoint, many references list the presence of rusty brown tufts of pubescence in the axils of major veins on the leaf lower surface of *Cornus officinalis*. Dirr (1990) indicates that the characteristic is not

Cornus officinalis (above and above right; right courtesy Rick Lewandowski)

sufficiently consistent to be much help, and Paul would not dispute. The struggling woody plants student best look elsewhere for help. The flower buds can aid in this respect, being covered by a very fine coat of rusty brown hairs; however, this characteristic is best seen on plants from bud set through early winter. After Christmas, the pubescence seems to vanish. Finally, the woody plants ID student could look to the bark for help. In general, *C. officinalis* has showier bark than its mostly European relative. In youth, the former shows dark shiny brown bark that could almost be described as cherrylike. The outer bark peels in horizontal strips and, if sited correctly for dramatic sunset backlight, it can be quite attractive, not unlike that of *Betula alleghaniensis*. Older plants show a more distinctly exfoliating bark with gray, brown, and rusty orange. The effect is still subtle, but then again, come January, most of us are looking for even the slightest bit of eye candy from the garden.

In the annals of horticultural esoteria, one can find reference to an extract of *Cornus officinalis* fruit in combination with cinnamon and Chinese chive having been used as an antimicrobial on food products. The Japanese cornel dogwood is best grown in USDA zones 5–8. Its native range runs through much of Japan and the southern two-thirds of Korea.

Cornus officinalis **'Issai Minari'** is described by Dirr (1998) as a presumed precocious-flowering selection.

Cornus officinalis **JC Raulston Arboretum form** is not a formal introduction of the arboretum, but a selection currently under evaluation. It appears to be a smallish branch sport of 'Kintoki' (see following) that grows wider than tall. If this turns out to be a stable trait, this form would be an outstanding selection for smaller gardens.

Cornus officinalis **'Kintoki'** was discovered in a cut-branch market in Tokyo and introduced to the United States by Barry Yinger through Brookside Gardens in Wheaton, Maryland. Plants produce heavy crops of brilliant sulfur-yellow flowers on stiff branches. The shiny dark brown exfoliating bark on young branches is as good as or better than some *Prunus* species.

Cornus officinalis **'Lemon Zest',** an introduction from the Morris Arboretum of the University of Pennsylvania,

Cornus officinalis 'Kintoki'

is described as a lemony-fragrant, bright yellow flowering form that is showier than typical for the species. According to Tony Aiello of the Morris Arboretum, the increased show comes from the longer-than-normal pedicels that hold the flowers out farther from the stem. The selection shows good exfoliating bark on branches up to 8 to 10 years old. Flowering time is typical for the species.

Cornus officinalis **'Y-Sp'** was found as a seedling variant by Japanese nurseryman Seijuu Yamaguchi. Leaves are medium green, splashed with irregular bands of bright yellow. The plant will likely do best in a bit of afternoon shade in warmer climates.

Cornus florida

GLOSSARY

acuminate having a pointed tip

adpressed lying flat and close to the stem or leaf to which it is attached

arcuate bow-shaped

calcifuge of a plant that normally does not grow in limestone soil

capitate resembling a capitulum, a head of flowers

cuneate wedge-shaped

cymose resembling or bearing a cyme, a flat-topped inflorescence where the central (terminal) flower opens first

corymbose resembling a corymb, a flat-topped inflorescence where the outer flowers open first

drupe a one-seeded fruit with a hard interior surrounded by a fleshy exterior, as in plums or cherries

epicormic shoots shoots that grow from a tree trunk

glaucous covered with a fine bloom

herbaceous of a plant that lacks woody parts

IBA indole butyric acid; a common synthetic hormone in rooting products

involucral bracts bracts that subtend a flower or inflorescence

K-IBA potassium indole butyric acid; a water-soluble form of a common hormone in rooting products

NAA naphthalene acetic acid; a common hormone in rooting products

paniculate resembling a panicle, a branched inflorescence

polyploid having more than the usual two sets of chromosomes

suffruticose of a plant with a shrubby base

umbellate resembling an umbel, a flat-topped inflorescence where all the flower pedicels originate from a common point

BIBLIOGRAPHY

Brickell, C. D., B. R. Baum, W. L. A. Hetterscheid, A. C. Leslie, J. McNeill, P. Trehane, F. Vrugtman, and J. H. Wiersema, eds. 2004. *International Code of Nomenclature for Cultivated Plants*. 7th ed. Leuven, Belgium: International Society for Horticultural Science (ISHS).

De Jong, P. C., and L. K. J. Ilsinik. 1995. *Cornus sanguinea* 'Midwinter Fire' and 'Winter Beauty' (in Dutch). *Dendroflora* 32.

Dirr, Michael A. 1998. *Manual of Woody Landscape Plants*. 5th ed. Champaign, Illinois: Stipes Publishing Company.

Krüssman, Gerd. 1984. *Manual of Cultivated Broad-Leaved Trees and Shrubs*, 3 vols. Portland, Oregon: Timber Press.

Rehder, Alfred. 1990. *Manual of Cultivated Trees and Shrubs*. 2nd ed, rev. Portland, Oregon: Timber Press, Dioscorides Press.

Reich, L. 1992. *Uncommon Fruits Worthy of Attention: A Gardeners Guide*. Reading, Massachusetts: Addison Wesley Publishing Company.

Sargent, Charles. 1894. *The Forest Flora of Japan*.

Trigiano, R. N., M. H. Ament, and W. T. Windham. 2002. A genetic study of pigmented *Cornus kousa* cultivars. METRIA 2002 Conference Proceedings. http://www.ces.ncsu.edu/fletcher/programs/nursery/metria/metria12/trigianoetal

Wilson, E. H. 1913. *A Naturalist in Western China*. New York: Doubleday.

Windham, M. T., E. T. Graham, W. T. Witte, J. L. Knighten, and R. N. Trigiano. 1968. *Cornus florida* 'Appalachian Spring': a white-flowering dogwood resistant to dogwood anthracnose. *HortSci* 33: 1265–1267.

Witte, W. T., M. T. Windham, A. S. Windham, F. A. Hale, D. C. Fare, and W. K. Clatterbuck. 2000. *Dogwoods for American Gardens*. The University of Tennessee Agricultural Extension Service Publication PB1670. 1–32. http://www.utextension.utk.edu.

Wyman, Donald. 1967. *American Horticulture Magazine* (July): 165–174.

USDA HARDINESS ZONE MAP

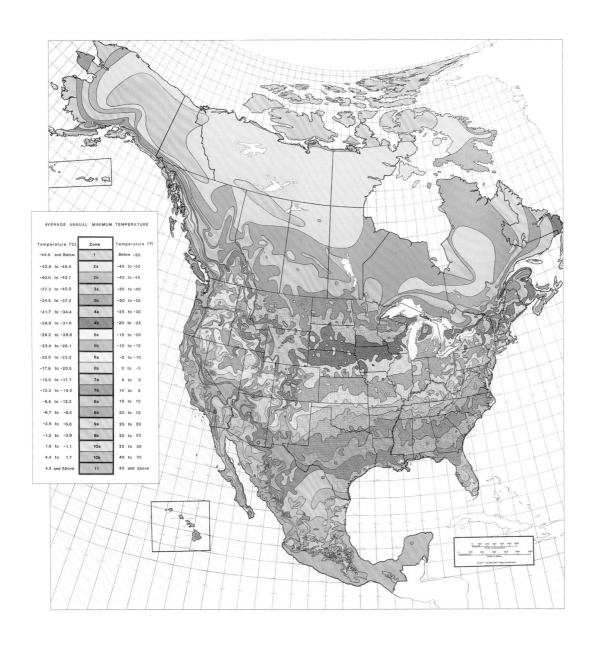

Temperature (°C)	Zone	Temperature (°F)
AVERAGE ANNUAL MINIMUM TEMPERATURE		
-45.6 and Below	1	Below -50
-42.8 to -45.5	2a	-45 to -50
-40.0 to -42.7	2b	-40 to -45
-37.3 to -40.0	3a	-35 to -40
-34.5 to -37.2	3b	-30 to -35
-31.7 to -34.4	4a	-25 to -30
-28.9 to -31.6	4b	-20 to -25
-26.2 to -28.8	5a	-15 to -20
-23.4 to -26.1	5b	-10 to -15
-20.6 to -23.3	6a	-5 to -10
-17.8 to -20.5	6b	0 to -5
-15.0 to -17.7	7a	5 to 0
-12.3 to -15.0	7b	10 to 5
-9.5 to -12.2	8a	15 to 10
-6.7 to -9.4	8b	20 to 15
-3.9 to -6.6	9a	25 to 20
-1.2 to -3.8	9b	30 to 25
1.6 to -1.1	10a	35 to 30
4.4 to 1.7	10b	40 to 35
4.5 and Above	11	40 and Above

INDEX

Abies balsamea, 27
Aesculus, 24
Alangium, 23
Arctostaphylos, 41
ash, 24
Aucuba, 23

bear berry, see *Cornus canadensis*
bear grape, see *Cornus canadensis*
Bentham's cornel, see *Cornus capitata*
Betula alleghaniensis, 210
Biblical Series™, see *Cornus kousa* Biblical
    Series™
bigleaf dogwood, see *Cornus macrophylla*
black fruited dogwood, see *Cornus sessilis*
blueberry, see *Vaccinium*
brown dogwood, see *Cornus glabrata*
bunchberry, see *Cornus canadensis*
Buxus 27

Calycanthus, 32
Camellia, 47
Caprifoliaceae, 24
Cephalotaxus, 27
Cercidiphyllum japonicum 'Amazing Grace',
    134
Cercis canadensis
   'Covey' (Lavender Twist™), 179
   'Silver Cloud', 134
Chinese dogwood, see *Cornus kousa*
Cornaceae, 23
Cornelian cherry dogwood, see *Cornus mas*

Cornus alba, 27, 28, 33, 48, 49–51, 58, 59,
    60, 61, 62, 67, 70, 72, 73
  'Albovariegata', see 'Argenteo-mar-
    ginata'
  'Allemen's Compact', 51
  'Argenteo-marginata', 51, 52, 56
  'Atrosanguinea', 51
  'Aurea', 51–52
  'Bailhalo' (Ivory Halo™), 52
  'Behnschii', 52
  'Bloodgood', 53
  'Chblzam' (Chief Bloodgood™), 53
  'Cream Cracker', 53
  'Crimizam' (Creme de Mint™), 53
  'Elegantissima', see 'Argenteo-marginata'
  'Gouchaultii', 53
  'Hessei', 29, 54, 68, 76
  'Kesselringii', 54
  'Regnzam' (Red Gnome™), 55
  'Rosenthall', 55
  'Ruby', 55
  'Siberian Pearls' 55
  'Siberica Bloodgood', see 'Sibirica'
  'Sibirica' 29, 54, 55
  'Sibirica Red Gnome', see 'Regnzam'
  'Sibirica Variegata', 56
  'Snow Pearls', 56
  'Spaethii', 53, 56
  'Staltouch' (Touch of Elegance™), 56
  'Stdazam' (Strawberry Daiquiri'®), 56
  'Variegata', 56
  'Westonbirt', see 'Sibirica'

Cornus alternifolia, 25, 33, 83, 84–86, 87, 89, 93
 'Argentea', 83, 86, 91
 'Corallina', 87
 'Ochrocarpa', 87
 'Umbraculifera', 87
 'Virescens', 87
 'Wstackman (Golden Shadows™) 20, 87
Cornus amomum, 55, 57–58, 60
 'Indigo', 58
 subsp. *oblique*, see *C. obliqua*
Cornus angustata 138–139
 'Elsbry' (Empress of China™), 139
 'First Choice', 139, 140
 'Ticrn' (Prodigy™), 140
Cornus ×arnoldiana, 64
Cornus asperifolia, 58
 var. *drummondii*, 58
Cornus australis, 59
 var. *koenigii*, 59
Cornus baileyi, see *C. stolonifera* f. *baileyi*
Cornus bretschneideri, 59
Cornus ×californica, 78
Cornus canadensis, 16, 17, 18, 19, 26, 27, 39–45
 'Downeaster', 44
Cornus capitata, 17, 140–141, 191
 subsp. *emeiensis*,141
 subsp. *emeiensis* 'Summer Passion', 142
 'Mountain Moon', 141
Cornus capitata × *C. florida*, 189
 'Floricap', 189
Cornus chinensis, 209
Cornus controversa, 17, 83, 84, 86, 87–90, 93
 'GrY-C', 90
 'Hakkouda-no-kagayaki', 90
 'Janine', 90
 'June Snow', 90
 'Kansetsu', 90
 'Marginata Nord', 90
 'Pagoda', 91
 'Pk-Mg', 91
 'Rag Doll', 91
 'Variegata', 91
 'Variegata Frans Type', 91
Cornus coreana, 81

Cornus elegantissima, see *C. alba* 'Argenteo-marginata'
Cornus emeinsis, see *C. capitata* subsp. *emeiensis*
Cornus florida, 15, 16, 23, 25, 26, 28, 29, 31, 32, 34, 35, 36, 37, 40, 45, 83, 84, 97–102, 139, 140, 142, 143, 185, 186, 187, 189, 190, 191, 192, 196
 '66', see 'Ozark Spring'
 'Abundance', 102
 'Alba Plena', 102
 'American Beauty', 102
 'Am-erika Touch-O-Pink', 102
 'Andrea Hart', 102
 'Andy Heart', 102
 'Angel Wings', 102
 'Appalachian Spring', 34, 102
 'Apple Blossom', 103
 'Ascending', 29, 103
 'Aurea', 103
 'Aureo-variegata', see 'Kingsville Form'
 'Autumn Gold', 103
 'Barton', see 'Cloud 9'
 'Bay Beauty', see 'Welch's Bay Beauty'
 'Belmont Pink', 29, 104
 'Big Bouquet', 104
 'Big Giant', 104
 'Big Girl', 104
 'Blonde Luster', 104
 'Bonnie', 105
 'Boyd's Willowleaf', see 'Salicifolia'
 'Cherokee Chief', 105, 119, 128, 130, 138
 'Cherokee Maiden', see 'Ozark Spring'
 'Cherokee Princess', 29, 106, 117, 130, 132, 137, 194
 'Chiaro Di Luna', see 'Moonglow'
 'Cloud 9', see 'Barton'
 'Comco No. 1' (Cherokee Brave™), 37
 'D-184-11', see 'Rutman' (Wonderberry®)
 'D-376-15', see 'Rutnam' (Red Beauty®)
 'D-383-22', see Red Pygmy®
 'Daybreak' (Cherokee Daybreak™), 108
 'De Kalb Red', 108
 'Dixie Collonade', 108
 'Dunnewell', 108

'Eternal', see 'Eternal Dogwood'
'Eternal Dogwood', 108
'Fastigiata', 29, 103, 108
'Fayetteville Columnar', 108
'First Lady', 108–110, 117, 120
'Flower Chief', 110
'Fragrant Cloud', 110
'Geronimo', 111
'G. H. Ford', see 'President Ford'
'Gigantea', 111, 116
'Gold Braid', 111
'Golden Nugget', 111, 117
'Gold Nugget', see 'Golden Nugget'
'Green Glow', 111
'Heistar', 111
'Hillenmeyer', 29, 111, 132, 197
'Hillenmeyer White', see 'Hillenmeyer'
'Hohman's Golden', 112
'Imperial White', 113
'Irving Cline', 113
'Jean's Appalachian Snow', 30, 37, 113
'Jessica's Bouquet', 113
'Juanita', 113
'Junior Miss', see 'Welch's Junior Miss'
'Junior Miss Variegated', 114
'Karen's Appalachian Blush', 30, 37, 114
'Kay's Appalachian Mist', 30, 37, 114
'Kingsville Form', 115
'Lanham's Little Broom', 115
'Lemon Drops', 115
'Little Princess', 116
'Magnifica', 116
'Mary Ellen', 116
'Miss Marion', 116
'Montpelier', 116
'Moon', 116
'Moonglow', 116
'Mr. Theodore', 117
'Multibracteata', 117
'Mystery', 117
'New Hampshire', 117
'October Glory', 117
'Ozark Spring', see 'Cherokee Maiden'
'Pacific Gold', 118

'Pendula', 29, 118, 168
'Peve Rhoode', 119
'Phillips Pink No. 1', 119
'Pink Autumn', 119
'Pink Blush', 119
'Pink Flame', 119
'Pink Princess', 119
'Pink Sachet', 119–120
'Plena', 120
'Pluribracteata', 120
'Poinsett', 120
'Prairie Pink', 120
'Prairie Snow', 120
'President Ford', 120
'Presidential', 120
var. *pringlei*, 120
'Prosser Red', 29, 124, 130
'Pumpkin Patch', 124
'Purple Glory', 108, 124
'Pygmy', 113, 116, 124, 130
'Pygmaea', 124, 126
'Rainbow', 120, 126
'Red Cloud', 126
'Red Giant', 126
Red Pygmy® ('D-383-22'), 126–128
'Reddy', 128
'Redleaf', 128
'Rich-red', 128
'Robert's Pink', 128
'Rose Valley', 128
'Royal Red', see 'Cherokee Chief'
var. *rubra*, 19, 29, 124, 128, 130, 138, 191
'Rutman' (Wonderberry®),130
'Rutnam' (Red Beauty®), 130
'Salicifolia', 130
'September Dog', 130
'Shadow's Littleleaf', 131
'Shadow's Plena', 131
'Sno-White', see 'Cherokee Princess'
'Snow Princess', 132
'Spring Grove', 132
'Spring Song', 132
'Springtime', 29, 130, 132
'Steele's Fastigiate', 132

'Sterling Silver', 132

'Stoke's Pink', 132

'Sunset' (Cherokee Sunset™), 132

'Sunset Aurea', 133

'Super Dogwood', 133–134

'Super Red', see 'Cherokee Chief'

'Sweet Charlotte', 134

'Sweetwater Red', 37, 105, 124, 130, 134, 195

'Tricolor', see 'Welchii'

subsp. *urbiniana*, 135

'Variegata', 135

'Weaver', see 'Weaver's White'

'Weaver's White', 135

'Webb's Red Cloud', see 'Red Cloud'

'Welchii', 111, 115, 119, 136

'Welch's Bay Beauty', 136

'Welch's Junior Miss', 114, 130, 136

'White Bouquet', 136

'White Catch', 136

'White Cloud', 137

'White Giant', 137

'White Love', 138

'Williams Red', 138

'Wills', 119, 138

'Willsii', see 'Wills'

'Wine Red', see 'Prosser Red'

'World's Fair', 138

f. *xanthocarpa*, 19, 29, 138

Cornus florida × *C. nuttallii*, 189–190

'Ascona', 190

'Eddie's White Wonder', 188, 190

'Ormonde', 190

'Pink Blush', 191

Cornus foemina, 62, 66

Cornus glabrata 59

Cornus hessei, see *C. alba* 'Hessei'

Cornus kousa, 17, 23, 25, 26, 28, 30, 31, 32, 35, 37, 84, 138, 139, 140, 142–147, 189, 191, 194, 195, 197, 198

'Aget', 148

'Akabana', 148

'Akatsuki', 148

'All Summer', 148

'Amber', 148

'Angela Palmer', 148

var. *angustata*, see *C. angustata*

'Angyo Dwarf', 149

'Autumn Rose', 149

'Avalanche', 150

'Baby Splash', 150

'Baier', 151

'Beni Fuji', 31, 147, 151

Biblical Series™, 158, 170, 173

'Big Apple', 31, 151, 154

'Blue Shadow', 31, 151

'Bodnant', 152

'Boltinck's Beauty', see 'Bultinck's Beauty'

'Bultinck's Beauty', 152

'Bonfire', 152

'Bush's Pink', 152

'Camden', 152

'Cascade', 153

'Cedar Ridge Select', 153

'Cherokee', 153

'China Girl', 30, 153

var. *chinensis*, 30, 31, 154, 155, 156, 157, 158, 160, 162, 170, 176, 180, 184

'Chiprizam' (Christian Prince™), 155, 166

'Claudia', 155

'Crème Puff', 155

'Doubloon', 155, 168

'Dr. Bump', 156

'Dwarf Pink', 156

'Ed Mezitt', 156

'Elizabeth Lustgarten', 156, 162

'Elmwood Weeper', 157, 182

'Emerald Star', 157

'Endurance', 157

'Fanfare', 157

'Fireworks', 157

'Flowertime', 158

Galzam (Galilean®), 158, 170

'Gay Head', 158

'Girard's Nana', 158

'Gold Cup', 158

'Gold Star', 158

'Greensleeves', 31, 160, 167, 174

'Greta's Gold', 160

'Grumpy', 160

'Hanros' (Radiant Rose™), 147, 160

'Highland', 161

'John Slocock', 161

'Julian', 162

'July Jubilee' 162

'Kalmthout', 162

'Kirkpatrick's Weeping', 162

'Kordes', 162

'Kreuzdame', 162

'Kristin Lipka's Variegated Weeper', 162

'Laura', 163

'Little Beauty', 163

'Little China', 163

'Luce', 163

'Lustgarten Weeping', 162, 163

'Madame Butterfly', 164

'Madison' (Crown Jewel™), 164

'Marble', 164

'Milky Way', 30–31, 164–165, 173, 180

'Milky Way Select', 165

'Minuma', 166

'Miss Petty', 166

'Miss Satomi', 31, 147, 148, 166, 168, 174

'Moonbeam', 160, 167, 168

'Moonlight', 168

'Moonsplash', 168

'National', 168

'Nell Monk', 168

'New Red', see 'Miss Satomi'

'Nicole', 168

'Parasol', 155, 168

'Par Four', 168

'Pendula', 168

'Peve Limbo', 168

'Pollywood', 168

'Prolific', 170

'Propzam' (Prophet™), 144, 170

'Rasen', 170

Raulston Selection, 170

'Repeat Bloomer', 171

'Rochester', 171

'Rosabella', see 'Miss Satomi'

'Rosea', see var. *rosea*

var. *rosea*, 172

'Rosemoor Pink', 172

'Rubra', 172

'S. Hoffen', 172

'Samzam' (Samaritan®), 166, 173

'Satomi', see 'Miss Satomi'

'Schmetterling', 173

'Schmred (Heart Throb™), see 'Miss Satomi'

'Select', 174

'Silver Cup', 174

'Silver Phesant', 174

'Silver Splash', 174

'Silverstar', 174

'Simpson #1', 174

'Simpson #2', 175

'Snowbird', 175

'Snowboy', 175–176

'Snow Flake', 176

'Southern Cross', 176

'Speciosa', 177

'Spinners', 177

'Square Dance', 31, 177

'Steeple', 177

'Summer Games', 177

'Summer Majesty', 177

'Summer Stars',178

'Sunsplash', 168, 178

'Temple Jewel', 179–180

'Teutonia', 180

'Ticknor's Choice', 180

'Trinity Star', 180

'Triple Crown', 181

'Tsukuba No Mine', 181

'Twinkle', 182

'Variegata', 182

'Victory', 182

'Viridis', 182

'Waterfall', 182

'Weaver's Weeping', 157, 182, 184

'Weberiana', 184

'Weisse Fontane', 184

'Whirlwind', 184

'White Dream', 184

'White Dusted', 184

'White Fountain', 184

'Wieting', 184

'Wieting's Select', see 'Witing'

'Willamette', 184

'Wilton', 184
'Wiltoni', see 'Wilton'
'Wisley Queen', 184
'Wolf Eyes', 172, 180, 184–185
'Xanthocarpa', 185
Cornus kousa × *C. capitata*, 191
  'Norman Hadden', 141, 191
  'Porlock', 141, 191
Cornus kousa × *C. florida*, see *C.* ×*rutgersensis*
Cornus kousa × *C. nuttallii*
  'KN30-8' (Venus™), 32, 198
  'KN4-43' (Starlight™), 198
Cornus macrophylla, 17, 25, 93–95
  var. *macrophylla*, 95
  var. *stracheyi*, 95
Cornus mas, 15, 16, 18, 19, 25, 26, 28, 70,
    201–208, 209
  'Alba', 205
  'Aurea', 205
  'Aureo-elegantissima', see 'Elegantissima'
  'Crispa', 205
  'Elegant', 205
  'Elegantissima', 205
  'Flava', 205–206
  'Golden Glory', 206
  'Grovemas', 206
  'Helen', 206
  'Hillier's Upright', 206
  'Jolico', 206
  'Lanceolata', 206
  'Macrocarpa', 206
  'Morris Arboretum', 207
  'Nana', 207
  'National Arboretum Variegated', 207
  'Pioneer', 207
  'Pyramidalis', 207
  'Redstone', 207
  f. *sphaerocarpa*, 207
  'Spring Glow', 207
  'Spring Grove', see 'Spring Sun'
  'Spring Sun', 208
  'Tricolor', see 'Elegantissima'
  'Ukraine', 208
  'Variegata', 204, 208
  'Vidubetskii' (Redstar™), 208

'Violacea', 208
'Xanthocarpa', see 'Flava'
'Yellow', see 'Flava'
Cornus nuttallii, 32, 34, 37, 185–187, 189, 190,
    191, 198
  'Barrick', 187
  'Boyd's Hardy', 187
  'Colrigo Giant', 187
  'Colrigo Wonder', 188
  var. *eddiei*, see 'Eddiei'
  'Eddiei', 188
  'Eddie's White Wonder', see *C. florida* × *C. nut-*
    tallii 'Eddie's White Wonder'
  'Goldspot', 188
  'Monarch', 189
  'North Star', 189
  'Pilgrim', 189
  'Portlemouth', 189
Cornus obliqua, 60, 64
Cornus oblonga, 60
Cornus occidentalis, see *C. stolonifera* var. *occiden-*
    talis
Cornus officinalis, 19, 209–210
  'Issai Minari', 211
  JC Raulston Arboretum form, 211
  'Kintoki', 211
  'Lemon Zest', 211
  'Y-Sp', 211
Cornus omiensis, see *C. capitata* subsp. *emeinsis*
Cornus omeiensis, see *C. capitata* subsp. *emeinsis*
Cornus paucinervis, 61
Cornus pumila, 61–62, 207
Cornus peruviana, 17
Cornus racemosa, 33, 62–64
  'Cinderella', 64
  Counties of Ohio™, 64, 66
  'Cuyzam' (Cuyahoga™), 64
  'Geazam' (Geauga®), 64
  'Hurzam' (Huron®), 64, 66
  'Jade' (Snow Mantle™), 66
  'Mahzam' (Mahoning™), 66
  'Muszam' (Muskingum®) ,66
  'Ottzam' (Ottawa™), 66
  'Slavin's Dwarf', 66
Cornus rotundifolia, 48

Cornus rugosa, 66
Cornus ×rutgersensis, 31, 37, 160, 191–192
    'Galaxy', see 'Rutdan'
    'Rutban' (Aurora®), 191, 192–193, 197
    'Rutcan' (Constellation®), 191, 193–194
    'Rutdan' (Celestial®), 191, 194, 197
    'Rutfan' (Stardust®), 191, 194–195
    'Rutgan' (Stellar Pink®), 191, 195–196, 197
    'Rutlan' (Ruth Ellen®), 191, 192, 196–197
    Saturn™, 197
Cornus sanguinea ,17, 27, 48, 59, 66–67
    'Anny', see 'Winter Beauty'
    'Anny's', see 'Winter Beauty'
    'Beteramsii', see 'Midwinter Fire'
    'Compressa', 67–68
    'Greenlight', 68
    'Magic Flame', see 'Winter Beauty'
    'Midwinter Fire', 68, 70
    'Mietzschii', 68
    'Variegata', 68
    'Viridissima', 69
    'Winter Beauty', 68, 69–70
    'Winter Flame', see 'Winter Beauty'
Cornus sessilis, 70
Cornus ×slavinii, 66
Cornus stolonifera, 27, 33, 48, 49, 50, 55, 58, 61,
        66, 70–72, 78
    'Bailey', see f. *baileyi*
    f. *baileyi*, 55, 72
    'Baileyi', see f. *baileyi*
    'Bergesson's Compact', 72–73
    'Bud's Yellow', 73
    'Cardinal', 53, 73
    'Cheyenne', 73
    var. *coloradensis*, 73–74
    'Elongata', 74
    'Flaviramea', 73, 74–75, 78
    'Garden Glow', 75–76
    'Hedgerow's Gold', 76
    'Isanti', 76
    'Kelseyi', 76–78, 79
    'Lutea', see 'Flaviramea'
    'Nitida', 78
    var. *occidentalis*, 78, 79
    'Rosco', 78

    'Silver and Gold', 78–79, 80
    'Sunshine' 79–80
    'Variegata', 80
    'White Gold', 80
    'White Spot', see 'White Gold'
Cornus suecica, 17, 39, 43–45
Cornus ×unalaschkensis, 39, 44,45
Cornus walteri, 80–81
Crataegus, 54
creek dogwood, see *Cornus ×californica*

Davidia, 23
Diospyros virginiana, 80
Discula destructiva, 32, 34, 35

Elsinoe corni, 35
Ericaceae, 17–18
evergreen Chinese dogwood, see *Cornus angustata*

Fagus sylvatica 'Roseo-marginata', 136
Ficus benjamina, 139
flowering dogwood, see *Cornus florida*
Fraxinus, 24

Gaultheria, 41
giant dogwood, see *Cornus controversa*
gray dogwood, see *Cornus racemosa*

Helichrysum, 10
Helwingia, 23
Himalayan evergreen dogwood, see *Cornus capitata*
Hosta 'Bressingham Blue', 76
hostas, 28
Hypericum, 32

Ilex, 32

Japanese cornel dogwood, see *Cornus officinalis*

kinnikinick, see *Cornus canadensis*
kousa dogwood, see *Cornus kousa*

Lonicera, 24

Mahonia bealei, 76
maple, 24
Microsphaeria pennicillata, 36
Microsphaeria pulchra, 36
Monarda, 36
Mt. Emei evergreen dogwood, see *Cornus capitata* subsp. *emeiensis*

Nyssa, 23

Oleaceae, 24

Paeonia, 28
pagoda dogwood, see *Cornus alternifolia*
Phlox, 36
Phyllactinia guttata, 36
Picea orientalis, 27
PJM Rhododendron, 156
Polygonatum odoratum 'Variegatum', 86
Prunus, 28, 211
Prunus mume, 47

red osier, see *Cornus stolonifera*
red-stemmed dogwood, see *Cornus stolonifera*
Rodgersia, 28
Rosa, 28

Rosa multiflora, 154
rough leaved dogwood, see *Cornus rugosa*

Salix alba 'Tristis', 156
Septoria cornicola, 36
Siberian iris, 79
snakeroot, see *Cornus stolonifera*
Stewartia, 32
strawberry tree, see *Cornus kousa*
Synanthedon scitula, 37

Tatarian dogwood, see *Cornus alba*
Taxus, 27
Thuja, 49
Tradescantia, 10

Vaccinium, 39, 41
Vaccinium angustifolum, 41
Viburnum, 24

Walter dogwood, see *Cornus walteri*
wedding cake tree, see *Cornus controversa*
western cornel, see *Cornus glabrata*

yang-mei, see *Cornus kousa*